THE KISS FROM THE CROSS

The Kiss from the Cross

Saints for Every Kind of Suffering

Ronda De Sola Chervin

CHARIS

Servant Publications
Ann Arbor, Michigan

Charis Books is an imprint of Servant Publications especially
designed to serve Roman Catholics.

Published by Servant Publications
P.O. Box 8617
Ann Arbor, Michigan 48107

Cover design by Paula Murphy, Hile Design and Illustration

93 94 95 96 97 10 9 8 7 6 5 4 3 2 1

Printed in the United States of America
ISBN 0-89283-849-3

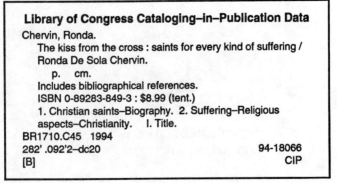

Library of Congress Cataloging–in–Publication Data
Chervin, Ronda.
   The kiss from the cross : saints for every kind of suffering /
   Ronda De Sola Chervin.
     p. cm.
   Includes bibliographical references.
   ISBN 0-89283-849-3 : $8.99 (tent.)
   1. Christian saints–Biography. 2. Suffering–Religious
   aspects–Christianity.   I. Title.
BR1710.C45 1994
282' .092'2–dc20   94-18066
[B]   CIP

Contents

INTRODUCTION

Meeting Christ in Suffering in the Spirit of the Saints

In the year 1991, my son Charles, took his own life, jumping off a bridge in Big Sur, California. In his letter to the family he told us that he thought it was pointless to endure the sufferings he was sure were inevitable in a world such as ours.

No suffering we had ever experienced before, such as asthma or cancer, could rival the unbearable pain for my husband and myself of our son's death.

For a year we wept and writhed, trying to dislodge in some way the terrible sword that had pierced our hearts. The prayers that we uttered in our grief seemed to come from a different, much more desperate place. They reached out not toward the light but, seemingly, catapulted into sheer darkness or backward toward the memory of the God rather than the living God.

Words from Scripture and from the writings of the saints which previously seemed a little extreme but yet understandable, suddenly seemed unbelievable. How could St. Paul really have penned the famous lines from Colossians 1:24-25: "It makes me happy to suffer for you, as I am suffering now, and in my own body to do what I can to make up all that has to be undergone by Christ for the sake of his body, the church."

Certainly I am willing to suffer for the church. Even cowardly me is sometimes willing to suffer for the church when I have no other choice, as in braving ridicule when defending Christian truth. But when St. Paul writes that he is *happy* to suffer, could he mean the type of sufferings we went through over the death of our son?

Or take such typical thoughts about suffering as these from St. Rose of Lima:

> If only mortals would learn how great it is to possess divine grace, how beautiful, how noble, how precious. How many riches it hides within itself, how many joys and delights! Without doubt they would devote all their care and concern to winning for themselves pains and afflictions. All men throughout the world would seek trouble, infirmities and torments, instead of good fortune, in order to attain the unfathomable treasure of grace."[1]

Coming upon it in my time of excruciating suffering over my son, I would wonder—suppose such beautiful lines are really just a sort of whistling in the dark. Suppose a saint is really just someone whose pain is so great that he or she has to invent some infinite meaning for it when really there is nothing but darkness and absurdity.

And when such broodingly melancholic speculations became overwhelming, I would escape into some secular novel to enter into another world. I sought a scene where I was not one of the characters, so I could rest from my misery. Sometimes I would find the Hound of Heaven waiting unexpectedly in the middle of the book.

Reading *Sula* by the black woman novelist Toni Morrison, I came upon a description of Pentecostal women at a funeral service, praising God loudly because "the only way to avoid the Hand of God is to get in it."[2]

Or, far into the *Raj Quartet* of Paul Scott about life in India during World War II, I came upon this stunner: "We must not forget the worst because the worst is our life and the rest is only history (our sanitized account). Between our life and history lies a dark valley where the rapt and patient shepherds of the flock drive us toward the God of forgiveness."[3]

And so I came to think that perhaps there was no escape from pain at all but that, instead, pain itself was the road into the heart of Christ where the holiness that had always eluded me might be found. And who better to journey with but the saints whose pilgrim-drink was that grail of intense suffering they eagerly sought at the hands of their beloved!

I decided to research the lives and thoughts of many types of saints who experienced suffering: saints for the addicted, saints for the depressed, saints for the fatigued, saints for the raped, saints for the unhappily married, saints for those in physical pain, saints for the frustrated, and several other kinds of suffering listed.

Among saints with certain afflictions I found a pattern that I, in my life, could ponder and imitate. For instance, reading of St. Elizabeth Seton's anguished fear for a teen son's salvation and well-being helped me understand that even saints cannot simply transcend the pain of fear for children by trusting in Providence. The pain is to be offered to Christ, not eliminated. Reading about holy stigmatists, such as St. Francis of Assisi, enabled me to overcome fear of a masectomy due to breast cancer by realizing the scar after my surgery would be like the wounded side of Christ, my Lord. I sincerely pray that you, too, will encounter saints whose example you can ponder and imitate.

Each chapter of *The Kiss from the Cross* relates the struggle of one saint, a sort of archetype, then goes on to add shorter reflections from the lives of other saints with the same cross. It concludes with suggested steps in meeting Christ in that particular suffering.

Will this be a depressing book to read? I think not. For me it brought courage and hope that in Christ and in communion with his saints, I could ultimately triumph over every kind of adversity. In reading about the sufferings of the saints, we also see the profound joy they knew, a foretaste of eternal happiness. My last chapter will show how we, too, can know more joy in the midst of grace-filled sufferings.

My Jesus, I beg you to hold us tightly as you bend down to kiss us from your cross. Let us feel your Sacred Heart beating against our wounded hearts, may we believe that our pain will bring us not to the hell of despair but to holiness on earth and infinite happiness in heaven.

ONE

Meeting Christ in the Suffering of Doubt

Oh man of little faith, why did you doubt? Matthew 14:31

Faith is the hope of things unseen. Hebrews 11:1

There are at least two main types of doubt that cause suffering. One is doubt about what is true; the other is doubt about what to choose to do. Sometimes these two experiences of doubt join together, sometimes not.

In the life of Thérèse of Lisieux there was never the slightest doubt about what she should do, for she wanted to be a Carmelite nun from her earliest years. But, as we shall see, there was terrible doubt of the truths of the faith—not the total doubt of a skeptic but rather a kind that can take place within the faith itself.

By contrast, once converted from worldliness, St. Ignatius Loyola had no doubts about the faith but some about his vocation. It was Ignatius who laid out for all future times the rules for discernment for Catholics uncertain about what to choose in life.

So we shall use Thérèse as our archetype for doubt of the faith, and Ignatius for the sufferings of indecision.

Finally we will conclude with an attempt to draw wisdom from the life and writings of a man who endured agonies from both types of doubt; Venerable John Henry Cardinal Newman. Doubt about whether the Catholic church was what she claimed to be, led to indecision about whether to remain an Anglican clergyman or to convert.

Interspersed among the main saints to be studied will be wisdom from the many others who endured one form or another of these common sufferings of doubt.

Generally, one would imagine that these sorts of doubts would flourish in the atmosphere of the university. Yet the accounts of doubt among the saints that seem to me to be more poignant are from the ranks of the less educated. Furthermore, the saint I have chosen as an archetype is from among that class who might be considered the least likely to be afflicted with doubt. St. Thérèse of Lisieux surrounded by firm devout church-people who never mingled with doubters of any kind.

Let us now turn to St. Thérèse to see how her encounter with doubt became an encounter with Christ.

ST. THÉRÈSE OF LISIEUX—A SAINT FOR DOUBTERS

Thérèse was born in 1873 to a family of pious lovers of Christ, fervent Catholics. She would never learn about philosophical doubt in the home setting but in the setting of those foolish people utterly outside the warm circle of family, friends, and the Carmel where she entered at an early age to join her beloved blood sisters.

I will not recount the well-known story of how this enchantingly lovable girl longed only to seal herself away in an enclosed convent that she might live only to please Jesus. That tale has been told to more Catholics than, perhaps, that of any other saint of all times!

I want, instead to concentrate on her interior life. Unlike many famous Carmelite saints, such as John of the Cross or

Teresa of Avila, the Little Flower was not at all given to ecstasies and raptures. There were one or two, but a great deal of her short life was spent in a state of aridity, a dryness which will be treated in our chapter on interior trials. Such aridity did not upset Thérèse. In her charming way she described it as an experience of Jesus asleep in the little boat of her soul.

It was only in the end times, before her death of tuberculosis, that Thérèse endured doubts of a critically painful kind. "If you only knew what frightful thoughts obsess me! Pray very much for me in order that I do not listen to the devil who wants to persuade me about so many lies. It's the reasoning of the worst materialists which is imposed on my mind. Finally, I offer up these very great pains to obtain the light of faith for poor unbelievers, for all those who separate themselves from the church's beliefs."[1]

Faced with a sense of uncertainty about something so fundamental as the existence of God, she would write in her journal:

It's very true that I don't see a thing. But I must sing very strongly in my heart: "After death life is immortal," or without this, things would turn out badly....

Down there, at the side of the chestnut trees, do you see that black hole wherein nothing is distinguishable? ... Well I am in a place like that, as regards both body and soul.... Ah! yes, what darkness! But I dwell there in peace.[2]

She described herself as a child "for whom the veil of faith is almost torn apart; yet it is no longer a veil—it is a wall reaching almost to Heaven, shutting out the stars. When I sing of Heaven's happiness, of what it is to possess God forever, I feel no joy; I simply sing of what I want to believe."[3]

As she lay dying in the midst of such doubt, she could write: "The very desires and intuitions of my inmost heart assured me that another and more lovely land awaited me, an abiding city... Then suddenly the fog about me seems to enter my very soul, and fill it to such an extent that I cannot even find there the lovely picture I had formed of my homeland; everything had disappeared."[4]

(And again:) Jesus... allowed pitch-black darkness to sweep over my soul.... I suffered it for months and am still waiting for it to end... it is a sunless tunnel... the voice of unbelievers came to mock me out of the darkness: "You dream of light, of a fragrant land, you dream that their Creator will be yours forever and think you will one day leave behind this fog in which you languish. Hope on! Hope on! And look forward to death! But it will give you, not what you hope for, but a still darker night, the night of annihilation..." He knows very well that although I had not the consolation of faith, I forced myself to act as if I had. I have made more acts of faith in the last year than in the whole of my life.[5]

Ida Goerres, in her sensitive insightful biography, explains that if we had not known of Thérèse's struggles with doubt we might have imagined that she was simply cradled in tradition and family piety with no relation to the storms of skepticism surrounding her in the world. Because of her doubt, she was forced to reach out to Christ from the depths, making her faith all the more beautiful. Goerres writes:

Thérèse transcended her own state of mind and her own feelings. She knew what was true and real whether or not she felt, understood, or experienced it. The Sun was in the sky, even if she were blinded. She had seen the radiant light; she knew she had seen it; and even if she no longer knew—it had vanished to such remote spaces—she still knew that she had known it once, and that would have to satisfy her. And so she wrote and prayed as if nothing had happened, as if her whole inner world had not been buried by an earthquake.[6]

In fact, even at her worst moments she told her mother superior that she would defend the truths of the faith with the last drop of her blood, that she didn't need to see heaven now if she could offer this suffering for poor sinners to see it in eternity.[7]

During this time of suffering doubt, Thérèse never changed her little way of love—always just as patient and sweet as when she was strengthened by the sense of God's presence. This steadfast love stands in contrast to the way many Christians in times of doubt will tend to hedge their bets by dabbling in sin or at least by taking it easy when it comes to sacrifice for others. It was part of Thérèse's heroic virtue not to change in the slightest so that few knew that she was undergoing a crisis of faith at all.

Of course, Thérèse was not the first saint to experience doubt. If we are to trust the mystic Venerable Mary of Agreda in her writings about the life of Mary, Mother of Jesus, the sense of loss of Jesus was first felt most poignantly by Mary when she could not find him during the visit to the temple. Mary Agreda likens her own seventeenth-century dark nights of doubt to this experience of Mary.[8]

St. Augustine, who went through so much skeptical doubt on the road to the Catholic faith, once in possession of Christ in the church wrote: "God is not a deceiver, that he should offer to support us, and then, when we lean upon him, should slip away from us."[9]

Gregory the Great wrote that "the disbelief of Thomas [the doubting apostle], has done more for our faith than the faith of the other disciples. As he touches Christ and is won over to belief, every doubt is cast aside and our faith is strengthened."[10]

Some of the deepest most consoling thoughts about holding on to faith in spite of the darkness of doubt can be found in the writings of St. John of the Cross. In the *Ascent of Mount*

Carmel the Spanish Doctor of the Church explains that we do not become more united to God on this earth through greater natural understanding but precisely through the darkness of faith.[11]

His teaching about the dark night of the soul is summarized by Federico Ruiz, O.C.D. in this helpful manner. The Dark Night of the Soul takes place among those who are somewhat spiritual and have enjoyed many special graces. Then comes a sort of living death where all impulses, plans and desires seem without any savor. God's purpose is to purify us from inordinate attachment to the egoism of self in all its forms. Because all seems covered in darkness and obscurity, our souls become purged and ready to receive all as a gift.[12]

Included in this Dark Night would be the truths of the faith which need to be grasped in a wholly supernatural way, rather than being simply a heritage or a matter of theological expertise. I find that it is vastly consoling to those having what seems like a crisis of faith after many years of fidelity to Christ in the church, to realize that this sense of darkness is truly God's work and not, instead, some form of punishment for one's sins and failings.

The darkness that feels like despair, as understood by St. John of the Cross, will be explored in our chapter on interior trials.

The experience of doubts about the faith, and revulsion against religious ideas and practices can be found most intensely in the life of St. Jane of Chantal (1572-1641) the disciple of St. Francis de Sales. A widow with several children, she was to found the Order of the Visitation.

For somewhere in the vicinity of forty years she struggled with doubts and feelings of abandonment. These she interpreted as a special call to utterly surrender to God, being willing to accept even the absence of any felt sense of his presence. In this attitude she was following the advice of her spiritual master, de Sales, who wrote in response to a nun who described feeling nothing, not even faith or hope, that:

> You do possess them, however, and very much so, only you don't derive any enjoyment from them. You are like a child, whose guardian does not allow him to spend all his fortune and so, although the money belongs to him, he cannot touch it... God does not want you to have control over your faith... except just enough to live on and to draw from in times of absolute necessity....
>
> Assure our Lord, even aloud or sometimes in song, that you are willing to endure a living death and be nourished as though you were dead, that is, without taste or feeling or awareness. In short, our Savior wants us to be so entirely his that we have nothing left and may be totally and unreservedly surrendered to the mercy of his Providence.[13]

Before going on to the subject of doubts of indecision, let us consider the following:

STEPS FOR MEETING CHRIST IN THE MIDST OF DOUBTS ABOUT THE FAITH

1. Continue to pray to the Jesus you knew before the onslaught of doubt, taking part in religious practices of the past.

2. Proclaim the truths of the faith, even sing of them. (It is remarkable how often the singing of holy songs is mentioned in the lives of the saints as a way to meet Christ in suffering.)

3. Engage in works of love of neighbor. In extending love we dwell in love, and abiding in love we dwell in God even if we don't feel it. This increases the love in our hearts so that after the crisis of faith, we will be even closer to God than before.

4. Understand doubt as a trial that will bring us to a new and greater level of supernatural faith, not dependent on any previous support we might have found in our own reasonings or the faith of others in the community.

5. Offer the sufferings of doubt for those who have never known God at all.

MEETING CHRIST IN THE SUFFERING OF INDECISION

Many holy saints have had difficulty discerning God's will in making choices. We might begin with St. Joseph who had to ponder in "fear and trembling" the choice of what to do about his alarmingly pregnant fiancée! We can see already in his case, how this just man prayed for light, avoiding all hasty decisions.

St. Benedict, the founder of the Benedictine Order, was a student in Rome at the end of the fifth century. He wanted to be a monk, but he was very unsure how to go about it. His remedy was to withdraw from active life to seek the will of God. This path is still being followed today by all those who make a retreat in order to better discern God's will for their lives.

During his time of testing, Benedict was helped by a holy monk and hermit, Romanus. In his own rule for monks, Benedict greatly emphasized the peace that will come with having recourse to the authority of the abbot when anxious about decisions. The abbot is said to hold the place of Christ for the monks.[14] The abbot, in his turn, must be a man of prudence. He must avoid excess in his decisions even though he must be ready to remove members whose presence would destroy the order of the monastery.

There are many stories about saints who thought they were destined to live in seclusion but who really were meant by God for a life that would be holy but more active in the world. Some examples would be St. John of the Cross, St. Anthony Mary Claret, and St. John Vianney. The latter so wanted to leave the vexations of his life as a parish priest that he ran away to the monastery, only to be turned back by the Holy Spirit. Most often the discernment to choose an active versus a wholly contemplative life comes through circumstances such as an unexplainable rejection by the stricter monastery.

Even though he himself did not have too many problems with indecision once he had made the most essential choice for Christ, St. Ignatius Loyola was the saint whose ideas about how to make difficult choices have become the most influential. Let us turn now to a brief summary of his life and wisdom about a suffering many Christians find extremely hard to plow through.

ST. IGNATIUS LOYOLA: TEACHER OF HOW TO MEET CHRIST IN THE SUFFERING OF INDECISION

Ignatius (1491-1556) was the youngest son in a noble family of thirteen children of the Basque country of Spain. He fought as a captain in the war of 1521 against the French, and, at twenty-six, was wounded in battle and suffered in captivity with a broken leg.

Before his injury, Ignatius had led the court life typical of noblemen of his era, marked by personal vanity, flirtations (if not worse) with women, games, and duels. Yet, in his favor it can be said that he was brave, uncompromising, enduring, understanding, astute, respectful of holy things, and forgiving of enemies.[15]

During his long convalescence with the broken leg there were no novels around about chivalry, such as Ignatius liked to read. His choice was between the *Lives of the Saints* and the *Life of Christ*. Out of sheer boredom Ignatius began to read these edifying books. During the inspirations that came with his readings he made his first big decision: to try to be a saint! This idea, so sudden and unexpected, vied with his former images of worldly glory. As he vacillated between these possibilities, he began to notice something about the choices:

> He observed that the ideas of sanctity were not merely good thoughts (because they were in conformity with the law of religion) but that they fortified his soul, consoled it, and so to say, filled it with solid food; whilst the ideas of worldly glory, though apparently agreeable during the time of his indulging in them, left his soul, on their departure, empty and unsatisfied.
>
> By this sign he was in the future able to distinguish what came to him from the "good spirit," from God or one of his angels, and what came from the "bad spirit." By this means, according to the testimony of those who gathered together the recollections of Ignatius, he definitely established the theory of the discernment of spirits which was to be brought to perfection in his Spiritual Exercises.[16]

The sickbed reflections of Ignatius, leading to the desire for holiness, were sealed by a vision of Mary and the Child Jesus, after which he was free for the rest of his life of all impure temptations, whether mental or physical.

Some Christians imagine that once a person makes a total commitment to Jesus, there is no future possibility of error about God's intentions. The lives of the saints do not bear out this hope. For example, although Ignatius was quite a decisive person, always eager to set out to do whatever seemed good to him, we can see that many of these decisions were not consonant with the destiny that God eventually revealed to him as his vocation.

For instance, immediately after his tremendous vision and full conversion he wanted to enter the Carthusians. But, after a time, he began to think that even this strict order was not penitential enough! He began to practice severe penances which ruined his stomach.

Next he decided to go to the Holy Land on a penitential pilgrimage in order to start some sort of order of his own to convert the Moslems of Palestine. In spite of various attempts, he would never personally organize a mission to convert the Moslems.

Knowing of these false discernments in Ignatius' own life should warn us not to imagine that we are being given some sort of infallible guide. The ideas of Ignatius about decision-making are most helpful, but complete certainty about choices concerning *various good possibilities* is not possible on earth. I emphasize the words "various good possibilities," because it is always possible to know with certainty that between an evil and a good choice, we must always avoid the evil one. We do not need to make a long retreat or go for spiritual direction to find out, for example, that sex outside of marriage is always wrong, but to choose between two good occupations may require much pondering.

During the first lap of Ignatius' journey to Palestine, he stopped at the Shrine of Our Lady of Montserrat and prayed all night. He gave his rich clothing away in exchange for that of a poor man and made a general confession. He also stopped at Manresa and lodged at a hospital where he nursed the sick and prayed seven hours at a time. He was unkempt and was mocked as a fanatic.

During this period of his life, Ignatius passed through a dangerous time of suicidal despair from scruples. He was fortified by supernatural visions. His prayer became rapturous, but he was also very ill. Originally thinking his vocation might be purely contemplative, he was forced to realize that it must also be active because of the desire that consumed him to convert others to greater love of God.

Entering back into normal society for this purpose, he realized that he would have to dress better, eat better, and also that he needed to learn more about the faith in order to teach well. He also prepared himself by compiling a draft of the Exercises he had composed to lead others in Manresa to union with God.

Here is a summary by one of his biographers, Fr. Henri Joly, S.J., of the plan of these exercises:

What is the book of the Exercises? A series of meditations, prayers, resolutions and pious actions, divided into several weeks, and arranged on a strict plan. As walking, marching and running are bodily exercises, so the different methods of preparing and disposing the soul to get rid of all its ill-regulated affections, and after having got rid of them, to seek and to find the Will of God in the ordering of its life, with the object of securing its salvation, are called spiritual exercises.

The first meditation convinces us that God is our leader and our end... and an examination of conscience, the indispensable preliminary to every pious action, shows us how far we are from realizing the inspiration of this idea... it would be an act not only of disobedience, but of ingratitude, to disregard his appeal for our loyalty.

We should not act like men who want to gain a military victory yet live happily without fighting. We must make up our minds resolutely to crush the obstacles to holiness especially affections which even if lawful are ill-regulated and so clash with the sacrifices necessary for the desired result.... We must... advance steadily and gently [in sacrifice], according to our strength from one step to another. During times of consolation we must make decisive resolutions so that in the time of desolation we may not fall.[17]

Most important of the decisions Ignatius wanted to help Christians make is the choice of a state of life.

If the man entering upon a course of the Exercises has not yet settled this, the moment has arrived for him to make his choice, by the light of these principles, i.e. checking to see whether a choice comes from God by noting the steady peace and joy that comes with an inspiration from God versus the immediate joy that leads later to weariness and darkness that comes with an inspiration not from God. If a person is already in a state of life he must fix on how he will make use of this state in life to serve God in a holy manner.[18]

Fr. Joly, of the Jesuit Order Ignatius founded, mentions that Ignatius himself in his anxiety about what way of life to choose had to make use of the basic Catholic tradition of frequent prayer, examinations of conscience, confession, Communion, meditation on the life of the Lord—for this places the soul in a good position to discern.[19]

An unusual aspect of Ignatian teaching is his view that one should find out which particular position of the body fosters good dispositions of the soul. When we pray in that position, we are letting the whole body share in the fruits of meditation.[20]

I mention this prudent concept of Ignatius about bodily posture because I believe there are many Christians who would spend much more time in personal prayer if they did not imagine it entailed kneeling at church. While for some the kneeler in a chapel is the best way because of the presence of Jesus in the Blessed Sacrament or because of long tradition and habit, for others lying in bed or taking a walk is a much better position for prayer since they feel so much more relaxed and happy.

During this time of preparation for the full use of his gifts in later life, Ignatius was eager to learn from many teachers and sat at the feet of Dominicans, Benedictines, and Cistercians. He developed, as a result of his ponderings, a special way to meditate, making use of the imagination in getting in touch with particular scenes from Scripture.

After quite a long stay at Manresa, Ignatius journeyed through Spain and Italy as a pilgrim, begging for food and lodging on his way to the Holy Land. Once arrived, he started telling spiritual leaders in the Holy Land about his plans for converting Moslems. They were frightened that the zealous Spaniard would bring down persecution upon the local Christians, and they encouraged him to leave after just six weeks! We might note that this shows that even very holy prayerful souls might learn the will of God through circumstances rather than immediate revelations.

On his return to Europe, Ignatius decided to devote himself to study even though he was past the usual age. He forced himself to learn Latin. Gradually he assembled a small group of male followers; before this time it had been mostly women of the noble classes who had followed his teachings. Subsequently he enrolled at the University of Alcala.

I think it is amusing to learn that at Alcala, and later at Salamanca, Ignatius was imprisoned for a short time for the "crime" of speaking about Christ before he had finished his studies. In those days there was much fear of heretical doctrine, and it was thought that one who could discourse so eloquently without benefit of formal learning might be one of those proud men and women who believed that they could proceed on the basis of private revelations alone.

Later he went to Paris to study for seven years. Here he formed a band of men, some of them his teachers. During the time of his schooling he did not give the exercises. He was afraid that it would lead to greater and greater mystical ecstasies which would distract him from study.[21] It is noteworthy that this decision to prefer studies to mystical ecstasy was made not on the basis of some special revelation but rather on the basis of commonsensical prudence, a means of discernment available even to the least mystical among us.

In fact, a close look at the life of Ignatius Loyola indicates that he made many a shrewd decision on the basis of a prudence. When off on a journey and summoned by the French Inquisition, he had a notary certify that he had set out to obey the order to return immediately. This prudent act contributed to his favorable judgment from the Dominican inquisitor in Paris, probably because flamboyant visionaries are rarely prudent. Out of high-handed disobedience such heretical visionaries would never return quickly to those they would regard as mere functionaries.

To help his disciples be sure about vocations postponed by years of wavering, he had them make the exercises.[22] When dealing with an advisee of a melancholy temperament, Ignatius told him to give up dreams of a hermit-like solitude which might increase this despondency. From such examples we can draw the conclusion that Ignatius did not recommend a solitary pursuit of God's will without the corrective of seeking the advice of others.

When Ignatius had finished his studies and had gathered followers who hoped to become missionaries to the Holy Land, he travelled with the group from Venice to Rome. During this trip decisions were made on the basis of a plurality of votes.

During this time Ignatius had a famous vision in which Christ told him to center his work in Rome. Jesus embraced Ignatius and told him he wanted him to be his servant, after which Ignatius named his group the Society of Jesus. It wasn't until 1538 that they decided to become a formal order. This came after meeting every night and sharing reflections and then voting. The final constitutions were not completed until 1550. The manner of taking the vote is interesting. "Each one was to consider the matter in private without consulting or advising any of his brethren; each one was, as far as possible, to remove from himself all his affections, all personal considerations, and picture to himself that he was working for other men, and had to give them for their benefit perfectly disinterested advice."[23]

In the rule of the Society of Jesus, obedience was central to right decision making, yet this was not to remove freedom of spirit. Obedience was to keep them from pride and to maintain enthusiasm and unity. The new Society, devoted to working for the advancement of souls through teaching, preaching, the Exercises, works of charity, catechesis, and confession, also voted unanimously for choosing one head to obey, subject to the approval and confirmation of the Holy See. In matters of great importance, however, the vote of the council would decide. The order was also devoted to following the pope in whatever mission he would wish to send them.

To elect the superior, they devoted three days to prayer and meditation. Ignatius was the unanimous choice, but he refused. They voted again, and he tried to refuse but one of the brethren said he must yield to God's will. Ignatius consulted his confessor and then yielded.

Immediately the members dispersed to missions as far away as Japan and China. In Rome, Ignatius worked for education of children, conversion of Jews, and homes for orphans and women who wanted to escape prostitution.

Members of the Society of Jesus were among the most influential at the Council of Trent. Ignatius helped mediate disputes between pope and prince, founded colleges and universities, and avoided ecclesial honors which would hamper the freedom of spirit and mission of his sons.

At the peak of success, he tried to resign but had to give in to the unanimous insistence of the Society that he remain as superior. After this he devoted himself to working on the constitution of the order.

Even though the constitution called for individual obedience, they also respected a person's doubts on a matter at hand by requiring such doubts be set forth.[24] When unsure what to write in the constitutions, Ignatius would offer Mass for the intention of light until he felt an irresistible force tending in one direction.

During his time in Paris, Ignatius had revised the exercises,[25] which proved so helpful to many in discerning God's will for their lives. An interesting book showing the influence of Ignatian spirituality on St. Francis de Sales was written by a French Jesuit priest, Francois Charmot.[26] It shows how the Exercises of St. Ignatius enabled de Sales on a retreat in 1604 to discern that he would found a religious order and to "see" the persons who would help in what would become the order of the Visitation nuns. The sisters of the convents were trained by de Sales to give the Ignatian Exercises to lay women.

De Sales was especially concerned that no one make decisions under a feeling of pressure, a likely sign of the influence of bad spirits. Consideration of wrong choices leads to distraction of heart, disgust of soul, and dissipation of interior faculties. Signs of the Holy Spirit include sweetness, ease, tranquility, courage, strength, and inspiration.

When our decision is the result of good spirits, we are indifferent to success and remain in peace when we have done whatever we can to forward our plan; but when evil spirits are involved, we are inundated with worry, bitterness, and pain. Fear and secrecy are also often present when such wrong decisions are being considered.

I wish now to just briefly refer to the decisions of a few other saints, confirming elements of the Ignatian method.

The life of St. Bernard was filled with difficult decisions—not only personal ones but matters involving the destiny of the entire church. To arrive at the right decision, Bernard combined fasting, prayer, and study of the merits of the case. Sometimes he had to decide the merits of two contesting popes! Often he was chosen as a consultant in the decisions of others since he was judged to be the holiest man of his time.

Catherine of Siena, who lived centuries before Ignatius, once asked Jesus how to know what ideas came from him and which from Satan. She heard this reply:

> If you ask me how you are to recognize what comes from the devil and what comes from Me, I answer that this is the

sign for your guidance—If the ideas come from the devil, the soul receives all at once a feeling of lively joy; but the longer the state lasts, the more the joy diminishes, and it leaves you in weariness, confusion and darkness.—But if the soul is visited by Me, the Eternal Truth, it is, at the outset, seized with a holy fear and subsequently receives gladness, sweet prudence, and the desire of virtue.[27]

From the life of St. Alphonsus Liguori we have this interesting anecdote. When Liguori's prospective order was very small and insecure, another newly founded order wanted to join with him. Though he had great personal reluctance because of previous difficulties with the leaders, he submitted the decision to the advice of the Bishop and spiritual director, and to common sense. The Bishop advised against the merger.

I cannot end this chapter on meeting Christ in the sufferings of doubt without reference to one of the most heartrending nineteenth-century accounts of indecision as displayed in the *Apologia Pro Vita Sua* of Venerable John Henry Cardinal Newman, the famous convert to the Roman Catholic faith from Anglican belief.[28]

Religious from boyhood, this brilliant scholar became an Anglican priest at a time when there was much controversy over whether the Church of England should be seen as really a branch of Protestantism or as the true successor to the early church, taking the place of a Roman church considered to have become the Antichrist through its betrayal of true doctrine and practice.

Newman was at the forefront of the party that held to the latter view, seeing the Church of England as apostolic. He deeply loved his work in the Anglican church as a preacher, scholar, and writer; and he was beloved of the people, who found in his sermons a call to holiness they had not known before.

Intent on proving the claims of the Church of England

against the doubts of Protestants and Roman Catholics, Newman began an intense study of the writings of the Fathers of the early church. By the year 1841, however, after years of intellectual struggle and indecision, he had become convinced that such research only strengthened the claims of the Roman Church! This led to a state of intensely painful indecision. How could he be sure he was now right, when before he thought he was right about the goodness of the Anglican way and now was convinced he had been wrong?

To add weight to his Roman convictions, in 1845 he wrote *An Essay on the Development of Christian Doctrine* which to this day is considered by many Catholics to be the best way of refuting the idea that certain Catholic teachings are untrue to the Bible and to the early church.

In this book Newman's basic distinction is between changes that constitute contradiction and changes that constitute development. On the basis of this distinction, he could show that the Roman Catholic teachings about Mary did not consist of idolatrous distortions of Scripture and early tradition but rather in *developments* of what was always present, like a seed.

So, by 1845, we find Newman overcoming his theoretical doubt about the claims of the Catholic church but still postponing the decision to leave the Anglican church. Even though he was the type of courageous man who would have to act consistent with truth regardless of the personal consequences, Newman dreaded hurting and unsettling many Anglican scholars, whom he dearly loved, by announcing his convictions about the truth of Roman Catholic claims. He believed that there was grace in the Church of England, even if Rome had the fullness of grace and truth. He feared that going over to the Roman church would bewilder followers shaken by their leader's seeming inconstancy. He feared they could not understand his theological reasonings and would simply begin to doubt all doctrine.[29] One of his prayers for the light of truth reflects this painful time of doubt and indecision: "O my God, I confess that Thou canst enlighten my darkness. I confess that Thou alone canst. I wish my darkness to be enlightened.... I hereby promise that by Thy grace which I am asking, I will embrace whatever I at last feel certain is the truth, if ever I come to be certain. And by Thy grace I will guard against all self-deceit which may lead me to take what nature would have, rather than what reason approves."[30]

Readers suffering from indecision about religious matters would do well to read Newman's Apologia to trace the long, thoughtful manner of this priest's search for truth, always combined with the most ardent prayer that nothing of his own weakness should mar his decision.

Finally his burning conviction that the Lord Jesus Christ wanted to meet him in the Roman Catholic Church of the apostles, led him to a conversion he would never regret. The courage of his decision, backed by such painstaking reasoning, brought countless others to the joy of the same choice.

The following steps on prudent decision making are based on the Ignatian Exercises:

STEPS FOR LIBERATION FROM THE SUFFERING OF INDECISION

1. Prepare for your decision by means of self-examination, repentance, confession, and penance.

2. Prayerfully decide that your sole interest is in God's will without reference to your own desires. To work up to such a sentiment it is necessary to meditate deeply on the passion of Christ, so fear of suffering does not dominate you.

3. Consider the various alternatives before you. As you imagine yourself making each of the choices, take time to test whether you experience a deep lasting joy at the thought of this path or whether, on the contrary, you experience a momentary elation followed by confusion.

4. Having chosen the path that seems to bring lasting joy, rest in thanksgiving to God.

5. This process is not a solo journey. It is made in consultation with an experienced director. Here is where the step of prudence comes in, for the mentor can easily detect rashness or irrational zeal. Yet the director does not make the decision for the retreatant. This must come from communion with God himself.

TWO

Meeting Christ in the Suffering of Being Exploited

*For though I am free from all men, I have made myself
a slave to all, that I might win the more.*
1 Corinthians 9:19

He who was free when called is a slave of Christ.
1 Corinthians 7:22

Many women feel exploited in the home. This feeling is on the increase nowadays when so many women work outside the house only to come back to many tasks not shared equally by husband or children.

But many men feel exploited also. They may experience unfair treatment at the hands of their bosses. The sense of oppression is increased nowadays when some married men come home to help with housework or the children, and they have little rest from labor.

Most people don't consider burdens to be exploitation unless the work that they must do is unjustly allocated, underpaid, or received with ingratitude. Since many of uswho wish to respond to what life presents in a Christian way feel ourselves to be stuck in exploitative situations, how are we to meet Christ in our feelings of chronic hurt and anger?

PRAXEDES FERNANDEZ—EXPLOITED YET FREE

Why pick a woman not yet canonized with a name unknown to most readers rather than some more famous medieval saint? I have chosen to tell Praxedes' story in detail because I believe that many homemakers will be able to identify with her so easily. And since I believe she will be beatified soon, you will rejoice in this great event of church history.

Praxedes (pronounced Prax-cee-dess) was born in 1886 into a family of mining engineers. She was one of twelve children, five of whom died in childhood. The members of her pious family loved the Mass and the rosary. They were known as peacemakers among their neighbors and as helpers of the poor.

Even as a child Praxedes wanted to help the poor and sick and loved to pray the rosary. "She was very obedient. Never did she question her duty in daily chores."[1] I imagine that some mothers reading this last sentence will be sure that Praxedes should be canonized!

The holy Spanish girl was always energetic. She helped her mother with housework, worked at the family bakery, tended the sheep, and worked in the garden. She was taught by Dominican sisters who testified at the process of investigation toward beatification that everything about Praxedes was willingness to help. She would give her lunch to the poor; and if someone hit her, she would not retaliate. She was very joyful, peaceful, and humble.

Praxedes loved flowers and poetry. She could play guitar, sing well, and folkdance. She especially loved to dance the *jota*. As a young woman she went to daily mass and then to wait on customers at the general store, with milking, cleaning the stables, cooking, sewing, baking, and weeding as additional tasks. She would take spiritual reading along when out in the fields.

In the midst of this busy life Praxedes found time also to be a catechist, a nurse of the poor, and an informal counselor to those with problems.

She enrolled as a Daughter of Mary and later in an archconfraternity started by the Passionist Fathers. These practices developed her lifelong devotion to the crucified Christ. Praxedes always made the stations of the cross, weeping as she went along, a highly recommended practice for anyone with a long-term suffering.

One friend of mine used to let out a deep sigh under each station, waiting to turn to the next one until she felt some comfort. Identification with Jesus makes us feel less alone in carrying our own crosses.

Once Praxedes was asked by a child, who was looking at a picture of Jesus extended from the cross embracing St. Francis, how Jesus could lean down so far if the nails held him to the cross? Praxedes replied that it was not so much the nails that held Jesus to the cross but love.[2]

This answer can be viewed as the motto of her own life. She would serve people with love not because they demanded it of her as an obligation (like a nail)—even though they did demand it—but for her own motive which was love.

Praxedes was much attracted to the Dominican sisters with whom she had studied. Nevertheless, she stayed at home motivated mainly by the desire to nurse her beloved sick father. Her parents wanted her to marry and Praxedes reluctantly agreed. She couldn't become a sister if she was to devote herself to the care of her father, whereas she could continue to help him as a married woman.

The pious young woman rejected several suitors who did not seem right to her. The reasons are characteristic. One was too miserly. She was afraid that if she married him she would not be able to give to the poor. The other was found to have another girlfriend in secret. I mention these refusals because they indicate that Praxedes had plenty of will to resist other's wishes when she chose to, even when her parents pushed for a match.

Finally at age twenty-eight, quite old for those times, she fell in love with a poorer man whom she thought worthy because of the goodness she saw in him. He was an electrician who could barely pay the rent for a few rooms. By that time Praxedes' own family had become quite well-to-do. This young man, Gabriel, was not very religious—doing only the minimum along lines of piety, but he attracted Praxedes even so.

Gabriel had a very bad temper and after their marriage, he became abusive. Only one year after their marriage when she was pregnant with their first child, he slapped her. He had become impatient with the extended length of the service on Good Friday.

"She accepted it with the meekness of a lamb, happy to resemble her Savior."[3] He also used to frequent a nearby bar and keep bad company. Their landlady told Praxedes' mother-in-law, who in turn asked her about it, but Praxedes said that all was fine.

Gabriel would repent of his flare-ups, but things kept getting worse. Finally Praxedes confided in her father and later in an uncle. Her uncle suggested that she tell her mother-in-law who in turn berated her son so sharply that he completely reformed and their marriage was never troubled by his temper thereafter. He also stopped visiting the bar. He continued to waste his meager salary on tobacco and taking his friends out to dinner, but this was minor compared to his previous faults.

Meanwhile Praxedes continued to pray constantly and with much affection, going to daily Mass and adoring Christ in the Blessed Sacrament. Jesus kept her company as she communed with him during her housework.

When the husband of Praxedes died in a train accident just after the birth of their fourth child, she was grieved deeply, especially for fear that he had died without having made a good confession. God sent her a sign that he was on the way to heaven.

Now begins the time of the direct exploitation of our saint. A widow with four children—five years and younger, with no pension or bank account[4]—Praxedes had to turn for help to family members who were now wealthy.

According to the wishes of her father before his death, any of the daughters who was widowed was to receive her part of the inheritance directly. But since he had not written down these instructions as was required by the law, Praxedes' mother adopted another plan. She was willing to take in Praxedes and her four sons into her home, where an unmarried sister Florentina lived; but she offered only room and board, and Praxedes began to help in the house in a way that became more and more servile.

The sister, Florentina, was the baby of the family and had always been coddled. She was a schoolteacher. Florentina did not like babies at all and resented the crying and mischievous noise of the four orphaned children. She also disdained housework.

This sister, one of the people giving a great deal of testimony at the process for Praxedes' canonization, testified that Praxedes became a servant, a Cinderella.

Before the elder sister's arrival with her boys, the family had had a servant. Not wanting to take care of such a large number of people, the servant soon left. Praxedes said there was no need to get another maid since she herself could take care of everything.

I could not find any completely satisfying explanation about Praxedes' reason for making herself a servant of the whole household. She would bring breakfast to her mother and sister in bed, then serve them other meals at the table (never asking her sister to help her) before she herself ate in the kitchen. She had to make clothing for her sons out of her father's old garments.

I would speculate that Praxedes' decision was a combination of several factors:

- She may have felt that having chosen to marry a poor man against the wishes of her parents, and therefore being left a penniless widow, she had no right to demand to be treated like a wealthy woman with servants of her own.

- Being a woman of considerable physical energy with a need to be constantly at work, she might have preferred such activity to sitting about idly.

- She may have decided that it was better to do all the work than to have constant bickering with her sister over such matters. As it was, her sister would criticize her about daily choices involving purchases and use of food, and lock up the cupboard to make sure Praxedes' children did not filch extras.

- In her love for interior prayer, she may have preferred the company of the Lord to long meals with her relatives during which, no doubt, there must have been much conversation at variance with the spirituality of Praxedes.

But her own answers are much more inspiring. Praxedes used to say, "The more we suffer with patience and love in this world, the greater will be our glory in the next."[5]

Friends of the family, questioned about this exploitation, always say that Praxedes wished to live as a servant. She said that she wished to be like Mary, a handmaid. Praxedes always said that going often to Mass helped her to help others better.

The only suffering she complained of was Florentina's demonstration of dislike for the children. An otherwise meek Praxedes was always assertive when she thought her children were being too harshly criticized for boyish antics.

Praxedes had a great love for Jesus in the tabernacle, and by 1931 when her children were older, she went to three Masses a day. She sometimes saw Jesus in the host.

By 1926 Spain began to suffer from the disputes between Catholics and anti-clerical communists. When priests could not enter houses to tend to the sick and dying because of the hatred for the church in those homes, they sent Praxedes to tend to them. Neighbors would always let Praxedes in, so loved was she for her charity to all in the town, regardless of their political attitudes.

One of her sons died in an accident; another became a Dominican priest, ministering in Los Angeles; another died during the civil war defending the faith.

During the great outrages characterized by public massacres of priests and nuns, this extraordinary woman refused to hear the communists curse, always saying that they just did not understand. She offered penances in reparation for the atrocities. She would give to the poor of the best food she could find, whether the people were Catholics or communists. Atheists used to say that if all Christians were like Praxedes, they would believe.[6]

During this time, Praxedes became a Third Order Dominican and did penance for victimizers of Christians. She had abhorred violence and begged the son who enlisted not to kill. "Don't tell me a son of mine is killing anyone. Brothers should not kill brothers."[7]

During the bloody street battles of the Spanish civil war it was impossible to get medicine. Many died from typhoid or intestinal infection. Technically, Praxedes died of such an infection, but in a way we could say she also died of exploitation!

The sick woman would drag herself out even when practically dead to carry water into the house because her mother and sister were afraid to go anywhere, and her son did not want to do "woman's work." She died in 1936, perfectly resigned, her arms in the form of a cross, with a faint smile on her face.

Praxedes was buried in a common grave because of the war, but afterwards many people experienced miracles after invoking her intercession. Everyone who knew her thought she was a saint—even her sister Florentina!

Do other saints have anything to say about exploitation or related issues? About convent life, St. Teresa of Avila wrote:

> And force your will to do the will of your Sisters in everything even though you may lose your rights... strive to accept work yourself so as to relieve your neighbor of it.[8]
>
> Imagine always being the servant for all and seeing Christ in all, and this way to better obey and respect them.[9] Whether carrying water or working among the pots in the kitchen, the presence of the Lord is always felt.[10]

Is this, then, a recommendation for acceptance of exploitation? I think not. After all, Teresa was no passive woman to be taken advantage of. She refused to live among the nonreformed sisters and assertively followed the Holy Spirit in forming her own. I believe that St. Teresa's point was that once within a chosen vocation, we should be generous and not petty, complaining, and demanding of our own rights. This is in light of the Pauline proclamation that begins this chapter: to be a slave for Christ.

Of all exploited holy ones the saint who seems to be the most touching to many is St. Germaine de Pibrac (1579-1601).

Here is a description of her life by Dana Black,[11] a mother impressed by how much the witness of this saint influenced her own children.

Little Germaine's mother died when she was a small child. When her father remarried, her stepmother took an extreme dislike to Germaine, partly because of the withered hand that she had been born with. In their poor family such a birth defect was a liability for housework and heavy farming.

Banished to the stable, sleeping on straw, and clothed in rags, Germaine had nothing to eat but table scraps. Not only that, her stepmother found taking care of the babies that came burdensome, so she took out her frustrations on Germaine in sarcasm, ridicule, beatings, and false accusations.

In her sufferings this real-life Cinderella turned to prayer, her only possessions a cross made of two sticks and a rosary made with a knotted piece of string. She never learned to read or write.

Miracles of God soon began to flow from this poor little girl's prayers. Villagers would hear beautiful music coming from the barn when Germaine was sleeping. Inside they saw the girl surrounded by light in a trance of rapture.

All day long Germaine tended the sheep. This was not a simple, pastoral occupation, for the wolves in the area could be deadly. She could also spin. She was devoted to the Mass, and would leave the sheep for her guardian angel to attend. Once during a storm the river overflowed making it impossible for Germaine to go to church. The villagers were astonished to see the river parting for the little saint. After Mass Germaine taught the children and the beggars about God's love.

Germaine's stepmother continued to beat her until she would collapse on the ground. Once, as she was falling, her apron opened revealing spring flowers even though it was winter. It was this miracle which converted the heart of Germaine's stepmother. She repented of her cruelty and invited Germaine to leave the stable and come back to live in the house. Very happy that her prayers for her stepmother had been answered, Germaine nevertheless preferred the simplicity and solitude of the stable. She died young, surrounded by angels.

Generally people who feel exploited will complain they are being treated like slaves. In view of this complaint, it might be thought provoking to end this chapter with a brief description of a man who called himself the "slave of the slaves": St. Peter Claver.[12]

St. Peter Claver was a Spaniard, born in 1581, who died in the New World in 1654. A brilliant student and a Jesuit, Peter longed not for academic work but to be a missionary in the colonies of the West Indies. Cartegena where St. Peter Claver was stationed after finishing his studies was one of the principal ports for the slave trade.

The slave trade had been condemned by the popes as a supreme villainy. It flourished even among Spanish Catholics, who thought that baptizing the slaves and keeping the families together was so much better than their treatment by other nationalities as to render the practice acceptable.

Peter was a shy man with little confidence, but he soon flung himself into the work of ministering to the black Africans who would arrive by the shipload at the piers of Cartegena. Shut up in the hold of the ship for months with a third of them dead on arrival, the slaves were in a condition too horrible for most priests even to view.

Claver, however, would organize the collection of food and medicine to give to the slaves. He had a band of interpreters so that he could evangelize them in their own languages. He would tell them about the crucified Jesus and show them how lovable they were in spite of their condition by the affection he would show them himself.

St. Peter Claver would also teach the owners of slaves to care for the souls of the blacks. He realized that the owners also had souls to be saved or lost by their treatment of the unfortunate slaves in their care. Once a year he would tour the plantations, living with the slaves to make sure they were not being ill-treated. The owners would complain about the amount of time wasted on preaching and singing.

It is estimated that St. Peter Claver instructed some three hundred thousand slaves.

Somewhat humorously, during a time of petty persecution, St. Peter remarked, "It behooves me always to imitate the example of the ass. When he is evilly spoken of, he is dumb. When he is starved, he is dumb. When he is overloaded, he is dumb. When he is despised and neglected, he is still dumb. He never complains in any circumstances, for he is only an ass. So also must God's servant be."[13]

I am sure that such sentiments nauseate some social justice activists. For me they illustrate the freedom of spirit that comes with *voluntarily* taking up a cross out of love for Christ. It marks the difference between a person enslaved by another human being and a person who defines himself or herself in any condition as truly Christ's slave.

STEPS TO MEETING CHRIST IN THE SUFFERING OF EXPLOITATION

1. Start with a generous willingness to help versus a grudging, lazy, egocentric approach to others.

2. Accept work as coming from God rather than as outrageous demands.

3. Confide your troubles to a religious person. For example, Praxedes eventually told her father, her uncle, and her mother-in-law about her troubles with her husband.

4. Do your work not to uphold an image of yourself as holy or because you are too weak to resist unjust demands, but out of loving goodness and genuine response to neediness. Praxedes gave to others not because of any conventional image nor because of others' demands, but freely. St. Germaine never complained not because she was a weakling, but because, through the love of Jesus, her own heart was full of love to overflowing.

   An indication that we are not helping out of goodness is when we say, "so-and-so makes me do it." No one really makes anyone do something since we could always leave a difficult situation. What we do is our choice even though a sense of duty to others may complicate matters as with Praxedes' desire to bring up her children in the family house.

5. Devote yourself to daily Mass, if possible, and to the passion, lying on the cross not because the nails bind but because you love with his love. Talk to Christ throughout the day.

THREE

Meeting Christ in the Suffering of Failure and Poverty

[Jesus] said, "Put out into the deep and let down your nets for a catch." And Simon answered, "Master, we toiled all night and took nothing! But at your word, I will let down the nets." And when they had done this, they enclosed a great shoal of fish... Luke 5:4-6

Consider the lilies of the field, how they grow; they neither toil nor spin;... O men of little faith. Therefore to not be anxious, saying "What shall we eat?" or "What shall we drink?"... your heavenly Father knows that you need them all.
Matthew 6:28-32

W hen you think of failure, what comes to mind first? Probably failure in achievement in the workplace, ending in grinding poverty and homelessness. Or maybe failure to win the love of another because a rival is deemed more attractive. Perhaps, as was the case of the suitors of many of the early women martyrs, the beloved prefers Christ to any human lover. Many Christians are plagued by such a sense of moral failure that they fall into despair. (The suffering that comes with this form of failure will be treated in another chapter under interior trials.)

Unfortunately, failure comes in many, many forms, sometimes for reasons that could not even remotely be considered one's own fault. Even though it is irrational, many people experience a sense of failure because they think they are ugly, or because they are poor or uncultured, or because of being barren or sterile. I hope that readers who are plagued by suffering for these sorts of reasons will find inspiration from the failure and poverty of the saints depicted in this chapter.

Sometimes, though, a sense of failure is clearly one's own fault. Consider good-looking, successful people who feel like failures because they compare themselves constantly to those who are even more successful or more attractive. Envy is one of the worst sufferings connected to a sense of failure. A person can feel like a failure, also, because of envy of those who seem to be much more holy.

Concerning all feelings of pain connected with failure and poverty, it is good to ponder the famous lines of the twentieth-century French Catholic writer, Leon Bloy: "There is only one failure, not to have been a saint."

Surely that was the conviction of all the saints. Let us explore what their lives can teach us. How did they overcome the bitterness that so often afflicts the poverty-stricken and those who feel like failures?

ST. BENEDICT JOSEPH LABRE: A GLORIOUS FAILURE

Perhaps you are not familiar with the life of St. Benedict Joseph Labre, a saint for street people, the very symbol of total failure in our society, and also in his.

The biography I am reading, by Agnes de la Groce,[1] begins with this beautiful line: "There is no more mysterious sweetness than the sweetness of sacrifice, and the dead wood of the cross has done more for men's consolation than all the living forests in the world."[2]

The utterly sacrificial life of St. Benedict Joseph Labre began in the plain of Artois in Flanders in 1748. Benedict was the firstborn son in a farming family. As eldest son he would be heir to the house, the stables, and the land. His mother would give birth to fourteen children after him.

Intensely religious from boyhood, his piety was also marked by a sense of justice. It was told in the process for his canonization that young Benedict reprimanded his mother for haggling with a dealer at the market, in case "the dealer might be paid less than was due him, or might feel called upon to lie."[3]

Benedict was noticeable among the other boys for his fiery temperament and his scrupulosity. These tendencies were encouraged by the teachings of an uncle, studying to become a parish priest, and much influenced also by tales of St. Francis of Assisi and his penitential practices. Benedict trained himself in the ascetical path by sitting far from the fire even in the coldest weather, and refusing dainty dishes.

At school Benedict was known as the best pupil ever to attend. He continued his education under the tutelage of another uncle who was a priest in a typical village where the curate was not only the spiritual leader but also the mentor in matters of agriculture and law. The priest was also a sort of town crier, announcing the most important news of the country each Sunday in church.

Most of these village clergy were rather worldly, enjoying the social life of the town with none of the burning zeal that characterized Benedict's uncle, a theologian and a holy man. Everyone expected the nephew to follow in the footsteps of the uncle.

The serious ardent youth, Benedict loved to spend time reading old books of spirituality in the library of the parish. Here he came upon treatises about the greatness of penance, inspiring men and women to expiate the sins of others by harsh sacrifices. The spirit must war against the flesh that tempts a

Christian to value bodily pleasure above the yearnings of the soul. Lauded were the deeds of those who tortured their flesh. Such writers were convinced that without their sacrifices many more people would be damned than those saved.

Such reading catapulted Benedict into a life of penance and a longing for the cloister. This desire, however, was contrary to the wishes of his family who wanted him to be a parish priest. Hearing a visitor describe the life of Trappist monks at the Abbey of La Grande Trappe, Benedict was thrilled by the description of monks praying all night, the abstinence in the refectory, the public confession of sins. Complete discipline, complete silence, complete renunciation, was the ideal of the founder, de Rance, who wrote, "It is not the man who has much who is rich, but the man who wants nothing."[4] Such a person would find everything in God.

Convinced that he was meant to be a Trappist, Benedict went home to ask for the blessing of his parents. They refused to let him go and sent him back to his uncle. The coming of the plague to Benedict's region brought peace to the young saint as he went out with his uncle fearlessly ministering to the sick and dying. While the priest was giving the terrified people the sacraments, Benedict would clean the bedridden and comb out the matted hair of the neglected children, also organizing relief efforts.[5]

When the uncle himself died of the plague, eighteen-year-old Benedict was sent to his maternal uncle to complete his studies. Now this man was completely given over to the Franciscan ideal: a parish priest with bare lacerated feet who gave away anything that came his way to the poor, spending the night praying in front of the tabernacle.

You might think that the austerity of the life they led together would sate Benedict's desire for sacrifice. But this was not the case. Moved by the harsh images of Christ crucified in contrast to the false gaiety and sinfulness of the people at carnival, he would yearn once more for the Trappist monastery.

His uncle advised as a compromise that he ask his parents' permission instead to apply to the Carthusians, less frightening to the popular imagination because there were several Carthusian monasteries in their own province. Finally Benedict was able to set forth to follow the dream so deeply imbedded in his fervent soul.[6]

Now comes the long saga of failure. The first monastery Benedict sought entrance to had recently been ravaged by fire, so he was refused entrance immediately for lack of space and provisions at the monastery.

Soon after, Benedict tried another Carthusian monastery at Montreuil. Again he was refused, this time because he seemed too frail and also because he was not proficient in chant. Placed in another parish church for further study, he was tormented constantly by the secular pupils who tried to get an attractive woman to kiss him. He fled the scene.

Back he went to the monastery at Montreuil, this time able to sing, only to be sent out again after a few weeks. The reason was some kind of profound misery that assailed his soul in this place, so great that the prior thought him not strong enough to remain.[7]

Benedict's biographer offers no further explanation at this point. The incident corresponds to the experience of many fervent single men and women who, believing themselves to be ideally suited to communal monastic life, try one order after another with no success. Something about monastic living appears to lead such Christians into severe emotional breakdown, whereas living in the world they are healthier even though they feel very unhappy for not fitting in with the compromise mentality of the world.

Benedict himself believed that his third failure to enter a penitential monastery was because he was called to the most extreme: La Trappe. How could his mother, unfamiliar with the sweetness that accompanies such penances, understand why her beloved son wanted to sleep at night on the floor with a log as a pillow? Finally it was the father who, convinced Benedict could never make a farmer or even a parish priest, agreed to his departure for the Trappists.

Travelling across uninhabited moors and forests, Benedict finally found the Trappist monastery. The abbot, however, decided that, rather than resign himself to the early death of a rash young postulant, he would refuse to receive this delicate youth. He kept him a while as a visitor and then sent him home!

Another failure! For a year Benedict humbly worked as a farm laborer. That winter, praying in his garret, the scrupulous ascetic began to berate himself for his failures, imagining that he had not tried hard enough to convince the Trappist abbot of his strength for the vocation. Looking out at the snow, he thought of all the souls that might be falling down to hell as fast as the snowflakes falling out of the sky because there was no one to offer himself for them in union with Christ on the crucifix.

Visiting the bishop for advice, he was told that he must instead follow his parents' wishes and again try the nearby Carthusians. Although he wished to stay with them, again the Carthusians sent him away as unsuitable and again he set off for La Grande Trappe.

And, again, failure. The abbot told him to wait! He never complained, only suffered, and journeyed toward still another Trappist monastery where they took younger men. It was an era full of anti-religious attitudes, and the state was busy shutting down monasteries, especially contemplative ones. Nonetheless, Benedict Joseph Labre, at twenty-two, was finally accepted at the Trappist monastery of Septfonts.

Judged to be a good candidate, devout and eager to work, it seemed as if Benedict's yearnings would finally be fulfilled. Yet, as it had happened at the Carthusian monastery, darkness began to close in on Benedict's soul. This trial of faith led to scrupulous fear of unworthiness in receiving Holy Communion.[8]

He would hold onto faith in spite of the despair that assailed his soul, but these heroic efforts could not conceal the growing weakness of his body and a mental condition that finally led the Abbot to fear for his sanity. Finally, Benedict himself was convinced that he did not belong with the Trappists, for in the midst of a fever he heard these words: "My son, God is not calling you to our order."[9]

Where was Benedict to go? In the midst of the darkness and the resignation, he abandoned himself to God's providence completely. After this act of surrender, he began to feel lighter of spirit.

Benedict wandered away from the monastery in the direction of Paray-le-Monial, the Visitation convent where St. Mary Margaret Alacoque had received the visions leading to an intensified devotion to the Sacred Heart. It should be noted that Mary Margaret had also experienced emotional distress to the point of being judged insane. At this monastery, one of the sisters took Benedict into the hospice. When he was better, he thought he ought to go on pilgrimage to Rome. In his day such journeys were much in favor, especially in times of personal trial and indecision.

Along the road, Benedict would stop to pray at the many holy places where saints had lived and died in order to venerate their relics. Light began to shine again in this troubled soul. In a sudden revelation, he realized that his vocation was to be a perpetual pilgrim—a sort of monk in the world. For this unusual call he received the approval of a priest seminary director.

Even though the great age of pilgrimages was over, every church had some kind of hospice where travelers could stay. In his day most of these visitors were tramps or criminals, and Benedict was often rounded up with such men by the police, to be put into prison. Out of humility Benedict soon called himself by the humiliating name of vagabond or beggar, rather than the noble title of pilgrim.

And he was treated the way street persons are today: ridiculed, tormented by urchins throwing stones at him, covered with filth and insects. In this way he felt that he could expiate for sins in union with Christ who was mocked, scorned, persecuted and subjected to physical suffering.

Benedict loved to repeat the words of Isaiah: "Surely he hath borne our infirmities and carried our sorrows: and we have thought him as it were a leper... He was offered because it was his own will... and was reputed with the wicked.... And they did spit in his face, and buffeted him... "[10] In this manner total failure became absolute success in love for Christ and for sinners.

There is not room in this chapter to detail the strange and moving life of Benedict Joseph Labre as he journeyed through France, Italy, Germany, and Spain from shrine to shrine. I will touch only on some exterior and interior highlights.

Wherever hospitality was given him, there would be healings, reconciliations, sometimes vocations. At first he would try to rid himself of vermin, but finally he allowed himself to be bitten, calling his body his carcass.

Though in the habit of judging others severely when he was a young man, Benedict finally came to see that sin was the result of men not knowing God's goodness. His joy grew as he saw the world not condemned but washed in Christ's blood. His own terrible scruples gave way to serene confidence.

When taking a small quantity of food offered him, he would say, "What we need is very little; all the rest goes to feed the worms."

In 1777, he made up his mind to stop traveling and settle down in Rome, living in a crevice in the Colosseum, eating at what would now be called soup kitchens but never begging, always praying his rosary or the breviary he still kept from monastery days.

Sometimes Italian artists used him as a model even for pictures of Christ.

As tourists passed through the Colosseum, he would mutter aloud what was on their consciences so that they would rush to sacramental confession.

During the night Benedict would walk around the moonlit Colosseum praying the stations of the cross for the sins of all humanity.

When he would walk in the streets each day, the other beggars would jeer at him, throwing stones, because he reproached them for their blasphemies. He was also thrashed by churchgoers who objected when he tried to escort their dogs out of the sacred premises!

Benedict loved to visit churches where the Blessed Sacrament was exposed. When carried away in prayer in church, he would be seen to levitate in ecstasy.

He liked to teach those beggar-pilgrims in the hospice who would listen though they also ridiculed him. Eventually they all changed for the better because of his influence.

Finally he was taken into a church hospice by a priest who recognized him to be a saint. Just before his death, Benedict became filled with joy and peace, free of all scruples. He died during Holy Week of the year 1783. Immediately all those who had mocked him, starting with the street urchins, started shouting that he, Our Lady's pilgrim, the "beggar of the forty hours," the "penitent of the Colosseum" the saint, was dead! Relic hunters came running to try to grab a piece of his rags or to cut off his beard.

Churches vied to have him buried within them. Some people of his quarter concealed knives in their clothing to kill any of the pious who might steal the body! At the funeral even cardinals and ambassadors came. And then began one healing miracle after another: of the blind, the paralyzed, the dumb. A visiting American Protestant minister, formerly an anti-

Catholic, was converted to the Catholic faith.

After Benedict's death many shared stories of his saintly goodness. Some told of his miracles. Those who had been his confessors were able to tell about his rich interior life. In fact, one of them, who was impressed by Benedict, had engaged him in long conversations and taken notes afterwards.

So great was the acclaim that Benedict's beatification cause was introduced the day after his death. His old father and mother back in Flanders would give their testimony about the holy childhood of the son whose way of life must surely have seemed to them to be a total failure. (Many are the saints who felt like failures during their lifetimes but whom we think of as roaring successes because of the enduring fruits of their sometimes thankless labors.)

We might start with the Holy Family. Jesus came to break the chains of greed and pride, to teach how possessions can oppress and darken the heart of humanity. He entered right away into a life of relative poverty and humiliation with his parents. What "a kiss from the cross" it must have been to have to see the royal child of prophecy come forth in a dirty cave! What misery to leave the security of the homeland for the journey into Egypt to save the life of the divine child.

St. Augustine reminds us that without the resurrection and the coming of the Holy Spirit, Jesus himself would be deemed an absolute failure. "Behold the glory of the cross! Once scoffed at by its enemies, it now adorns the head of the Emperor."[11] This was a reference to the fact that a cross adorned the crown of the Christian emperors.

St. Benedict, the founder of the Benedictine Order, had several major failures. First, there was a group of monks who begged him to come and be their abbot but then could not abide his holiness and the strictness of his direction. He responded by leaving, shaking the dust off his feet, telling them to "Look for an abbot after your own hearts. As for myself, I will stay with you no longer."[12]

This failure led Benedict not to give up but to form his own monastery with his handpicked disciples and leaders he could train. The story illustrates how failure often leads to a better venture.

Later on, St. Benedict's new monastery became so popular as a center of spirituality that it aroused the jealousy of the local priest. The envious cleric induced women to dance near the monastery to tempt the monks. Again Benedict, now fifty, left with several young monks to start afresh.[13] Just before he died, he foretold the destruction of his monastery by the Lombard hoards.[14]

St. Bernard, who became by his sixtieth year the greatest miracle worker of the twelfth century, sought after by multitudes including popes and kings, knew the sorrow of failure as well.

He had successfully preached a crusade to save the Holy Land, thinking such a cause would deflect the energies of the princes of Europe from wars between Christians. The crusade ended in defeat, a loss attributed by Bernard to the sins of the crusaders, including rape and looting.[15] For this failure he wept bitter tears.

His own monk-secretary betrayed him by secretly using the seal of St. Bernard to promote the careers of evil men.[16] Bernard called this period of his life "the season of disgrace."[17] Theodore Ratisbonne, one of his biographers, believed that the failure of the crusades was redeemed by the salvation of the souls of violent soldiers who at least were meritorious in dying for the Holy Land. God used the death of these crusading knights to rid Europe of perpetrators of feuds.[18]

In retrospect such analysis of God's providence can seem contrived, but we find ourselves trying to decipher the signs of the times whenever disaster results from a seemingly good historical initiative. Think of the speculation about God's will that went on in the middle of the American Civil War! To believe that some good can come even out of great evils reflects our faith in a God who alleviates even the unforeseen consequences of what we undertake.

Are there no examples of female saints who failed? Certainly many are to be found among the saints who had to mingle in the politics of the day. St. Joan of Arc might be considered the most famous of holy women who died in the belief that the cause she was fighting for was hopelessly lost. How could she realize that ultimately the powerful men who condemned her to the stake would be remembered in history largely because they failed to recognize the sanctity of a peasant maiden?

A different type of failure for a woman is someone who has been featured recently as a pro-life saint but could also be a patroness for all girls and women who feel like failures because they are deemed ugly. This is Blessed Margaret of Castello, who died in 1320.[19]

Margaret was the first child of the chief family of the Italian town of Metola. The whole city awaited the birth, preparing for the gala celebration. To the horror of her parents, a little baby girl was born who was blind, lame, dwarfed, and hunchbacked.

So unhappy were her mother and father that they pretended she had died at birth and kept her in the servant's quarters. When she grew older, they were afraid she might reveal the secret. So they had her walled up in a chapel in the forest as if she were an adult hermitess. Enthralled by the Eucharist and by the special graces she received, Margaret came to forgive her parents and also to experience the interior beauty of her own soul.

Eventually her parents took her to faraway Castello hoping for a miraculous cure. When she remained in unhealed ugliness, they abandoned her in the church to fend for herself. Blind Margaret joined the beggars, finally becoming a Third Order Dominican. She brought the beauty of family reconciliation to those she stayed with and healing to those afflicted with disease. In this way, worldly failure was turned by God into supernatural glory. How resplendent will all our bodies be on that great day when body and soul will be reunited in heaven!

Even saints considered to be attractive by their friends, could know failure concerning self-image. Handsome St. Teresa of Avila is reported to have said to the painter of the famous portrait of herself: "My God, you've succeeded in making me look ugly!"

Sometimes we feel inferior because we do not receive the same mystical gifts others have in abundance. Concerning this type of "failure" St. Teresa wrote that we should not envy others. All that counts is to do God's will. We should not wish for visions because we cannot know if we could bear the terrible trials that go with them.

In his biography of St. John of the Cross, Fr. Bruno writes of the seeming failure that characterized the last period of his life.[20] John had always prayed that, in imitation of Christ, he might be regarded as worthless and despised by all. God answered his prayer.

Toward the end of his life, he was deprived of all influence in the order he had helped found. In answer to a more specific prayer, he died in terrible pain at a convent where no one honored him. Fr. Bruno explains that such desires distinguish the quest for honor and dignity from the holy folly of the cross. Paradoxically we attain true psychological liberty out of mystical love for Christ in his sufferings.[21]

Describing a chapter meeting of the order where some hoped John would be elected provincial, the saint foresaw his treatment. "I shall be thrown into a corner, like an old rag, an old kitchen cloth."[22] His prophecy was fulfilled because he was willing to fail by not having any office in his order rather than acquiesce to the policies of higher-ups with whom he disagreed.

He was then sent off to Penuela—a very solitary poor monastery far from all his closest friends. It was of his experience in this monastery that he penned one of the most famous lines of all: "Where there is no love, put in love and you will draw out love."[22]

Failure would follow him to the end. Some enemies accused him of kissing a nun through the grille when he had really laid his hand on a wound in her neck to heal her.[23] On this spurious basis, they tried to throw him out of the order.

Becoming gravely ill, he was sent to a convent in Ubeda where he could be treated by a doctor. There he was given the worst room. The prior forbad the monks to tend him and he suffered terrible pain. Later the prior repented in tears. John of the Cross died saying he hoped to be saved not by his deeds but by the merits of Jesus Christ.

Of all saints of poverty, the one who seems to be the most touching to many is St. Germaine de Pibrac. I have described her life in the last chapter about exploitation. The image of the little girl living in a stable eating scraps from the table yet surrounded by radiant light and heavenly music is not, of course, an invitation to ignore social justice in favor of prayer, but still a historical proof of the way God's grace can overcome conditions of utter destitution.

A great failure-saint of quite a different type was Blessed Francis Libermann (1802-1852).[24] A brilliant boy, the son of a rabbi of a town in Alsace, Jacob Libermann followed the example of some of his brothers in becoming a Catholic. His greatest desire was to become a Catholic priest. In spite of his epilepsy, he was accepted as a candidate in a French order. Close to his ordination he had such a violent seizure that he was told he had no chance to fulfill his wish. Francis' disappointment was agonizing, leading him to the edge of despair.

Libermann's failure to become a priest led to the highly gifted young man's being utilized in the order as a sort of purchasing agent and general errand boy. Yet so deep was his spirituality that eventually he would become the informal spiritual director of many of the future priests at the seminary. Finally his health was deemed sufficiently under control that he could be ordained. What would have come of his life had he not accepted his failure with no abatement of his will to serve Christ in any capacity?

Many think of John Henry Cardinal Newman as a marvelous success. Renowned as an Anglican, when he was received into the Catholic church, he met with all kinds of failure. The branch of the Oratorian Fathers he founded in England was plagued by dissension, finally splitting into two houses in veritable rivalry with painful accusations going back and forth for decades.

Newman was begged to found a university in Ireland for Catholics so that Irish young people of the upper classes would not lose their faith while studying at Oxford. Years and years were spent in plans that never worked out to his satisfaction. In his last decade of life he was made a cardinal, but only after many years of suspicion by Roman authorities based on misunderstandings.

Moving to the twentieth century, we consider the failures in the life of Venerable José Maria Escriva. After the Spanish Civil War, it seemed as if all this priest's work in building Opus Dei foundations for students and other laity was lost. His university dwelling was in ruins and his disciples scattered. Escriva's attitude was that his work was God's work and so it was up to God to make it prosper.[25] So he restarted his work with even greater effort—also, always prayer. His later success was phenomenal.

STEPS IN COPING WITH FAILURE AND POVERTY

1. Accept setbacks or poverty as part of God's providence.

2. Avoid blaming others for your failures as if they were more powerful than God. After all, nothing can happen without God's permissive will. Ask for the grace to forgive those who stand in your way.

3. If convinced that some path is God's will, keep trying until God makes a particular goal absolutely impossible.

4. Identify your failure with the failure of Jesus, the God-man who was rejected by the people of his own village, by the religious leaders of Jerusalem, by Pilate, by the mobs paid to choose Barabbas instead, and by all those through the centuries who hear of him but refuse to follow him.

5. Pray that Jesus would give you the humility of the saints: to want only to succeed in love of God and neighbor.

FOUR

Meeting Christ in the Suffering of Fear

Even though I walk through the valley of the shadow of death, I shall fear no evil. Psalm 23:4

Perfect love casts out fear. 1 John 4:18

The word "fear" is mentioned in Scripture so many times that you would think it was another name for being human. Think of all the types of fear: fear of one's own death and the death of loved ones; fear of violence; fear of losing a job; fear of illness; fear of losing the love of those upon whom you are most dependent; fear of making a fool of oneself; fear of the loss of God's love through sin (such fear will be treated under interior trials) or of the fatal consequences of the sins of loved ones; fear of losing one's faith; and finally that most difficult fear to overcome, a free-floating anxiety without known cause.

You can easily add to my list. After describing the life of one saint who had many different kinds of fear, I will bring in the insights of other saints concerning fears you might find particularly upsetting.

BLESSED FRANCIS LIBERMANN: A SAINT
FOR THE FEARFUL

Something about the life of Blessed Francis Libermann, the Hebrew-Catholic nineteenth-century saint, has been given in our chapter about failure. Here I wish to describe him in much more detail for he is a wonderful model of meeting Christ in the suffering of fear so paralyzing and also humiliating to many Christians.

My account is based on the book *A Light to the Gentiles* by Adrian L. Van Kaam, C.S.Sp., the famous spiritual leader and Christian psychologist of our time who is a member of the order renewed by our saint: the Holy Ghost Fathers, also called the Spiritans.[1]

Jacob (later called Francis) Libermann was the fifth son of an important Jewish rabbi and his wife who lived in Saverne in Alsace. He was born in 1802 with a feeble body but a spirit that very early showed itself to be highly intelligent, glowing, and painfully sensitive. Van Kaam describes this "quivering awareness" as his greatest blessing and also his heaviest burden.[2]

Jacob was especially perceptive about the difficulties of the Jewish community living surrounded by Gentiles. Both groups hated their differences and carried on vendettas over shrewd business practices. Jacob interiorized all the fear that characterized an atmosphere where a Jew walking outside the shelter of his own street could be ridiculed and persecuted without redress.

He grew to feel that Jews were not like other people. Others were gay and light-hearted. They dressed in their best finery on Sunday mornings and went in crowds to a large stone building from whose rooftop sprang a massive tower. The building with the tower was marvelous indeed, but his father had spoken about it with such aversion that it now became for him a dark and threatening symbol of the hated other-world that lay outside his home, that terrifying world where one felt small and miserable as if he were always losing his way.[3]

Once Jacob ran into a Catholic funeral procession on the street. Terrified, he fled into a store and ran under the counter, cowering with fear. Meeting a priest in the street, Jacob darted over a wall and ran across a field.

Even among his own family and friends he was something of an outsider for he was too weak to play in the games of the other children. They would tease him for his frailty. This led to a twitch in his face he could not control. In his fear he would lean on his eldest brother.

When Jacob was eleven his beloved mother died, leaving him exclusively to the care of his father, a terribly serious man with one burning interest: that his sons should become as dedicated to the Jewish Law as he was. So strict was this Rabbi that when a member of his congregation killed a flea on the Sabbath because it had bitten him, he was given a penance of thirty days on bread and water!

At the same time, Lazarus Libermann gave his boys a strong example of charity, for he would house and feed the needy and charge nothing for educating poor students. Lazarus had a deep love for Jacob whom he saw as more than any of his sons destined to continue his life goals.

For many years he kept Jacob next to his side, forming him into a scholar of the minute details of the Law and the commentaries. Van Kaam is convinced that this shut-in atmosphere and the pressure of his father's ardent but smothering love caused much anxiety in the boy who had to repress constantly any desire for a freer, more merry childhood.

Many years later as a spiritual director, Francis (Jacob) would tell sensitive young men that rather than envy unrefined individuals who suffer less, they should realize that sensitivity was a gift of God bringing much pain but also a chance to grow in perfection at a swifter pace.[4] He would also give ample freedom to anyone under his authority, for he was sure that it was wrong to try to change others through dominance. He preferred to affirm their virtues and pray for their flaws of personality to gradually diminish.

From these days of suffocation under the authority of his strong-willed father can be traced the unbearable fear Jacob would experience all through his life whenever he had to resist the illegitimate demands of others. Those in healing ministries of our time are well aware of how much anxiety in the present can be traced to patterns of childhood involving severe physical or psychological punishment for minor offenses.

On the positive side, Jacob's long study of Jewish teaching led him to an abiding belief in the infinite transcendence of God, the worship of whom was central, always more important than any other matters that so easily preoccupy most men and women.

It is easy to imagine the horror of such a rabbi when he had to watch one son after another leave the safety of the Jewish world to go to study in the city. Away from his supervision his sons would not only mingle with Gentiles but also enter into the religious beliefs of the enemy by becoming Christians. One after another of his sons would forsake the love and security of the ghetto for the attraction of that alien figure: Jesus Christ.

It began with Samson, the eldest. Developing a disgust with rabbinical studies, Samson decided to go to Straussburg to become a doctor. He would attend the services at the synagogue from time to time, but he found that he could not pray anymore.

Marrying a Jewish girl with similar problems with orthodox Judaism, he began to look into the Gospels, finding his way to the Catholic church. Hearing the news later that year, the old Rabbi dressed in mourning and declared his son dead. This was the custom among the religious Jews of the time and is still done among Orthodox Jews of our day. The shock also led Lazarus to increase his pressure on the younger sons to cling to their hereditary religion.

It was the custom in Jewish life that when a scholarly boy had learned all he could from the local rabbi, he would be sent to a large city to sit at the feet of a still greater teacher. At twenty-two, Jacob was sent to Metz with the hope that his brilliance and piety would compensate for the deed of the traitor brother, Samson.

As he travelled on foot to Metz, however, the young man experienced not longing for further study but a delightful joy in being released from the heavy hand of his father. The plan was that the young man would study with a rabbi who had been a former pupil of his own father. A hearty welcome, including room and board, was expected.

To Jacob's surprise, the rabbi greeted him instead with cold formality. This unloving approach froze Jacob with such fear that he found a room for himself and never returned to the teacher his father had chosen for him.

The atmosphere of the school for rabbinic studies has been portrayed humorously but with basic truth in the movie *Yentl* with Barbra Streisand as the heroine-hero. Although steeped in tradition, many of the students came from backgrounds much more open than Jacob's to contemporary culture.

Soon he was devouring books his fellow seminarians discussed such as those by Enlightenment authors Rousseau and Voltaire! Rationalism began to destroy the piety instilled in his boyhood, and Jacob was assailed by doubt. Especially he would lie awake wondering if the miracles in Scripture were fabrications. Gradually, he adopted the view so prevalent in the wider society of his time that what mattered was to believe in God and love one's neighbor, not to be tied down by old-fashioned religious traditions.

While presumably studying for the rabbinate, Jacob spent most of his time learning languages and reading the classics. A turning point came when a fellow student asked him to help with the Hebrew of a particular text. The text was the Gospels! Reading the New Testament for the first time, Jacob was greatly taken with the personality of Jesus though skeptical about the miracles. Still he had to admit that such a figure as Jesus was so different from what the Jewish mind could conceive that the claim to divinity was intriguing. Could anyone but a god be that sublime? Was it possible to invent such a figure?

Meanwhile two other older brothers had become Catholics with the help of Samson! Repelled but also shaken, Jacob decided on the one thing he felt sure about: he was not destined to become a rabbi. At the suggestion of Samson, he decided to go to Paris to see what other vocation in life might appeal to him.

On the way he stopped at home to find his father tired and old, tortured by the news of his sons and terrified at what he might find had happened to Jacob, the favorite. He had been informed that his beloved son was spending more time on Latin than on Hebrew. Concealing his doubts, Jacob allowed his father to believe that he was still a firm believer in Judaism and got the cherished permission to go to Paris to study.

A visit to his brother Samson on the way to Paris perplexed him mightily. Torn between orthodox Judaism and freethinking, what was he to make of the serene joy of Samson and his wife, such convinced practicing Catholics? Samson gave Jacob a letter of introduction to the famous Dr. Drach, a former rabbi, now a Catholic scholar. This letter would accompany his father's letter on the journey and introduce him to Deutz, the chief rabbi of Paris.

The conflict boiling within began to show itself in physical symptoms, beginning with migraine headaches. These abated only when his brother Felix, living in Paris, started telling him of his conversion to the Catholic faith.

Soon Jacob made a first visit to both the Rabbi and the Hebrew-Catholic scholar. Though both treated him with kind solicitude, Jacob found that he had not sufficient belief to enter into the rabbinic studies the Jewish scholar suggested. He did think he might find it worthwhile to visit the Catholic seminary where Dr. Drach said he could do research in peace.

Sequestered in a gloomy room with old tomes to read, full of despair and dread, Jacob suddenly "fell to the floor and cried out to the God of Abraham, Isaac, and Jacob." Echoes from the Psalms formed themselves on his dry lips. Crushed in defeat, he prayed as he had never prayed before. Like a drowning man clinging to a piece of driftwood, he raised his head and adjured Yahweh to lead him into the light.

"All at once, with a burst of glory it was there. 'I saw the truth... faith flooded my mind and heart.'"[5]

Convinced now of the reality of the God of Scripture, the God of creation who entered history accomplishing supernatural miracles, Jacob was able to read about Christ with belief in the miracles, the resurrection, and even the Eucharist.

Jacob experienced overwhelming joy and happiness as he approached his baptism. Suddenly just before the ritual, the image of his father came to mind so strongly that agony wracked his spirit. A brief recollection of his dead mother, whom he sensed approving his baptism, calmed him.

During the exorcism ritual that accompanies Catholic baptism, a thrilling tremor passed through Jacob like a magnetic shock. "When the holy water flowed over my head... it seemed to me that I was in another world, in the center of an immense ball of fire. I no longer lived my natural existence; I neither saw nor heard what was happening around me... I actually became a new man. All uncertainty and anxiety vanished immediately. I felt a courage and supreme strength for keeping the Christian law; I felt a quiet affection for everything that belonged to my new religion."[6] Jacob took the baptismal name of Francis.

Did he live happily ever after? Interior peace, yes. Emotional calm, no. Immediately after his baptism, thinking to become a priest, Francis began to notice that some of the seminarians entertained anti-Semitic prejudices against him. They would eye him suspiciously and wonder about his motives. One day, after a troubling conversation with such a skeptical student, he thought about his father, who had not been told of his favorite son's baptism. With this came an overwhelming epileptic seizure, floods of anxiety and faintness.

It was humiliating to be seen in public, holding onto the wall to avoid falling down as epileptics do. Francis had to summon up all his confidence in God to continue at the seminary in spite of the ridicule of some of the healthy, strong young men around him. Going to pray early in the morning before the Blessed Sacrament was a source of peace.

Readers who are paralyzed with fear in public situations, especially when called upon to speak, should ponder the courage of Venerable Francis and ask his intercession.

Meanwhile Francis thought it necessary to write a letter to his father, trying to explain what had led him to Christ. Opening the return letter, pain rushed through his head. As he read, he turned grey and swayed as if he would faint. "You are damned forever... cast out like a leper... Come back... you are my last hope... return to your house... to the arms of your old father before he dies...."[7]

Surrendering himself immediately to God in his crisis, Christ came into his soul in a new way of such mystical power that he could easily resist his father's agonizing claims. He wrote a long loving letter to the old rabbi who died two years afterwards in great grief and bitterness of soul.

But before Francis could be ordained a priest, he began to suffer from more and more severe epileptic seizures with paralyzing headaches. This caused him to be fearful that he could never achieve the goal of the priesthood he longed for so much. In his terror he would hold the figure of Jesus in his mind continually.

Then came the worst kind of fits: "A wild shock ripped through his body, coursed down his limbs, and then concentrated on his head. A screaming whistle competed with the buzzing roar in his ears, and every object in the room took on extravagant proportions. With a horrible cry he lurched forward, swayed, and fell to the floor with a sickening thud."[8]

By means of prayer Francis was able to retain his peace of heart right after this attack, but then came an onslaught of fears that his father's curse caused the fit to prevent him from ever being a priest. Since an epileptic could not be a priest, what was to become of him? What life could such a man lead?

The seizures came one after another leaving him writhing on the floor. The agonies he went through make him a model for other sufferers of nervous ailments. He endured the fear and held onto faith through all his anxieties. He would come to call his illness his beloved malady for it was his way of sharing in the sufferings of Christ.[9]

After much forbearance, it became clear that Francis could not continue toward the priesthood. Since he did not want to go back to the world, he was given odd jobs to do, as explained in our chapter on failure. Gradually he became the advisor of many seminarians who leaned on his compassion and wisdom.

Fear did not leave the heart of Francis. Instead he learned how to bring his fear into prayer so that it could not paralyze him. The extent of the struggle can be measured by the fear Francis had of crossing bridges lest he throw himself off.

Ultimately Francis recovered sufficiently from his epilepsy to become a priest. He was also able to attract disciples to his plans for a missionary order which was to merge with the Congregation of the Holy Ghost.

This man so torn with anxiety was to become deeply loved for his example and for his teaching about how to surrender to the providence of God. Venerable Francis Libermann died in 1852 to be united to the Prince of Peace in whose arms he will never know fear again.

About nervousness, fear, and anxiety Venerable Francis himself was to write to someone receiving spiritual direction from him:

> You must forget about those nervous spells; ignore them, don't keep track of them. The thing that did me more harm than anything else was the anxiety, the restlessness, the precautions. In moments of stress we have to shake off such jittery feelings and forget ourselves, refusing to be gripped by anxieties. We must deal firmly with such emotions and be supremely indifferent about our ability to bear our affliction well or badly.[10]
>
> Gently put the brakes on the imagination and the feelings that are too strong.... slow up a bit on your external activity, so as to lend a peaceful and ready ear to the grace of the Holy Spirit who is in you.[11]

We will now turn to wisdom of the saints about certain fears we are particularly prone to.

For many Christians, fear of losing financial security is one of the most acute of anxieties. You will be surprised to know that St. Ignatius Loyola says that we should be so surrendered to God's will and trusting in his providence that we are not downcast at the loss of sources of income. Perhaps you think, "Well, that was fine for him, he didn't have a family to support." That sort of thinking leaves out the fact that Ignatius was the father of a whole religious community who spent the last years of his life devoting most of the hours of the day to handling the accounts!

Instead of scorning such holy advice, we need to pray for the greater faith in God that will enable us to trust in times of uncertainty.

In our chapter on physical pain we will go into much detail about enduring the pain itself. Here we want to mention something about fear of pain which can be just as trying.

St. Teresa of Avila had much reason to fear illness since there was never a day she was without pain.[12] The Spanish saint suffered from ringing in the ears, headaches, and constant stomach disorders leading to daily vomiting. Nonetheless, she wrote: "We could be deceived by worry about our health. Furthermore, worry over our health will not improve our health. This I know."[13]

A deep-seated fear of death affects many choices that we make. We can take heart in the struggles of two of the most famous believers of all times: King David and St. Peter.

David's fears in the face of so many implacable enemies are eloquently recited in the Psalms. His remedy was to fling himself into the arms of God, remembering past rescues: "He reached from on high, he took me, he drew me out of many waters. He delivered me from my strong enemy, and from those who hated me; for they were too mighty for me. They came upon me in the day of my calamity; but the Lord was my stay. He brought me forth into a broad place; he delivered me, because he delighted in me (Ps 18:16-19).

I love the last phrase "because he delighted in me," signifying the childlike trust David had in his Father-God.

David believed that God can best calm our fears when we stop our frantic activity to "be still and know that I am God" (Ps 46:10 RSV).

Quieted in his presence, we can say with David and with Jesus on the cross: "Into thy hands I commit my spirit; thou hast redeemed me, O Lord, faithful God" (Ps 31:5 RSV).

Of St. Peter's fears we have documentation in the New

Testament. It was Peter who was afraid he would sink in the waters when Jesus called out to walk toward him (Mt 14:30). Because of his fear for Jesus and for himself, he tried to stop Christ from going up to Jerusalem for the Passover (Mt 16:22). Three times Peter denied that he knew Jesus out of fear of being taken himself (Mt 26:69-75).

The remedy, in all cases, for Peter's fear was his calling piteously out to Christ to save him, either from the waters of the lake or from the misery of his denial of his Lord when Jesus needed him most.

We read in the First Letter of St. Peter: "Cast all your anxieties on him, for he cares about you" (1 Pt 5:7). Peter knew all about fear and worry, and yet still advised absolute trust.

St. John Chrysostom, a great Father of the Church, lived in times when fierce battles were fought over matters of doctrine. His enemies would often threaten him with death to the point of dragging him through the streets in an effort to torture and destroy him. With this in mind, his polished words on the subject bear pondering: "There is only one thing to be feared... only one trial and that is sin. I have told you this over and over again. All the rest is beside the point, whether you talk of plots, feuds, betrayals, slanders, abuses, confiscation of property, exile, swords, open sea or universal war. Whatever they may be, they are all fugitive and perishable. They touch the mortal body but wreak no harm on the watchful soul."[14]

About fear of old age St. Augustine once wrote: "When men wish for old age for themselves, what else do they wish for but lengthened infirmity."[15]

St. Anthony the Great consoles us with this adage: "As the body must be born after completing its development in the womb, so a soul, when it has reached the limit of life in the body allotted it by God, must leave the body."[16]

Some of the most beautiful writings about meeting Christ in fear of death come from the pens of the martyrs such as Blessed

Robert Southwell: "Ah fear, abortive imp of drooping mind; self-overthrow, false friend, root of remorse... ague of valor... love's frost, the mint of lies."[17]

And the martyr St. Thomas wrote, "I will not mistrust God, though I shall feel myself weakening and on the verge of being overcome with fear.... I trust he shall place his holy hand on me and in the stormy seas hold me up from drowning."[18]

In *The Interior Castle*, St. Teresa of Avila says that after experiencing the spiritual marriage the soul "has no more fear of death than it would of a gentle rapture."[19]

St. Francis Cabrini, so fearless in other ways, had a horror of drowning at sea. This she was obliged to overcome when the Pope himself asked her to leave her native Italy to go to America and minister to the needs of Italian immigrants who did not understand enough English to be helped by the English-speaking clergy. Perhaps St. Francis Cabrini would have been consoled by the lovely line of St. Thomas Aquinas "As sailors are guided by star to the port, so are Christians guided to Heaven by Mary."[20]

Before ending this chapter, I want to make good on my promise to include some advice from the saints about a malady little understood but often felt: free-floating anxiety. The strange-sounding name for this type of fear comes from the fact that whereas most fears involve a definite, somewhat fixed cause such as fear of being battered or fear of pain, many people experience another kind of fear where they do not know what is frightening them. It seems as if they are fearful about everything, a tendency to anxiety floating around ready to hit on any reason no matter whether it be rational or irrational.

Whatever the remote causes in the past for such anxiety that psychologists may unearth in personal therapy, it is good to reflect on the remedy suggested by most great spiritual writers and encapsulated in these passages from St. Francis de Sales: "The point of our heart, of our spirit, of our superior will—

which is our rudder—must incessantly look and tend perpetually to the love of God, its Creator, its unique and sovereign good."[21]

When this is true, we have much less anxiety about any possible danger in our daily lives, for we have not pinned our hopes on things of the earth but only on things of heaven which cannot fail us.

De Sales taught further that:

> If a soul seeks the means of being delivered of its evil for the love of God, it seeks that with patience... tranquility, awaiting its deliverance more from the goodness of God's providence than from painful industry or diligence.
>
> If it seeks deliverance because of self-love, it will press forward and be ardent in the quest for means, as if this good depended more on itself than on God... if it does not quickly receive what it hopes for, it enters into great anxieties and impatience... anguish and distress with a failure of courage and of strength so great that it seems its evil no longer has a remedy.[22]

It is hard to imagine that a man would write so well of this malady if he had not experienced it himself.

St. Margaret Mary Alacoque who had to suffer many interior trials of anxiety and also much rejection was told in a locution by Mary: "Fear nothing. You shall be my true daughter and I will always be your good mother."[23]

STEPS IN OVERCOMING FEAR THROUGH TRUST IN CHRIST

1. Admit the extent of your fear in prayer to God, crying out from the depths for courage. Repeat the words of Jesus:

"Father, if it be possible, let this cup pass from me; nevertheless, not as I will, but as thou wilt" (Mt 26:39).

2. Renew your faith, perhaps by reciting the Creed, to remember that what you fear to lose is less valuable than God himself and eternal life where you will find what you might seem to lose on earth.

3. Cry out to Christ to help you in your fear, picturing his hand reaching out to you on the waves of fear, as he did with St. Peter and with Blessed Francis Libermann.

4. Instead of spending time analyzing your fears, seek times of peaceful interior prayer, preferably before the Blessed Sacrament. You might repeat often the words of Jesus on the cross, "Into your hands I commend my spirit."

5. To prevent fear from overpowering you to the extent of paralyzing your will to do what would otherwise be good, ask Christ to give you a conviction that you are never alone and that he will be with you at the exact time of your feared future trial.

FIVE

Meeting Christ in the Suffering of Frustration

Be angry, but sin not; commune with your own hearts on your beds and be silent. Offer right sacrifices, and put your trust in the Lord. Psalm 4:4-5

Blessed are those who hunger and thirst for righteousness, for they shall be satisfied. Matthew 5:6

Let all bitterness and wrath and anger and clamor... be put away from you... and be kind to one another, tenderhearted, forgiving one another, as God in Christ forgave you. Ephesians 4:29-32

Frustration has many names; most of them sound like feelings, as in the phrases: "Don't give me any *grief*," or "I can't stand any more *aggravation*." We want to growl or grind our teeth when our cherished plans meet with opposition from enemies or even simply unfavorable circumstances. How often those who cannot cope with frustrations meet these setbacks with muttered or barked curse words!

Causes of frustration can seem infinite in number: lack of love, insufficient education, unemployment, problems with the boss, obnoxious behavior of children, terrible weather conditions, broken mechanical devices, traffic jams, crowded living space.

To Christians who are peaceful either by temperament or by well thought-out prudence, the irritability, anger, and rage of choleric personalities seems irrational and even amusing. How could someone stamp his or her feet over a delay or kick a harmless washing machine for its "sin" of breaking down after the owner has abused it for years!

But to the angry Christian trying desperately to become peaceful—a contradiction in itself—frustration is one of the most upsetting and painful aspects of daily life, compounded by deep humiliation over inability to overcome so visible a fault of character.

From the vividness of the description of frustration, have you guessed it is a special misery of the author of this book?

ST. ALPHONSUS LIGUORI: A SAINT FOR THE FRUSTRATED

Born in 1696 to a noble military family in Naples, Alphonsus was one of the sons of a swashbuckling sea captain, who wanted his sons to be just like him.[1]

Imagine the father's distaste in finding that Alphonsus was from birth unusually small, weak, and asthmatic. It is also easy to picture the effect on the boy of his father's constant rejecting ridicule for failings completely beyond his power to change. Let us consider this early perpetual wound as the first frustration of Alphonsus, that nothing he could do could make his father love him.

As the lad grew up, his father realized that there was no way to make Alphonsus into the military type of his desires. Since Papa Liguori had noticed that the boy was brilliant, he sent him to the university to study law. Alphonsus did splendidly. However, unlike most gifted students of the time, his intellectual interests could never distract him from an overwhelming empathy for the plight of the poor and a horror of the injustices inflicted upon them by society.

While pursuing the career his father had mapped out for him with ample gratification to his pride, he began to "hear" Jesus calling him in prayer to a life more dedicated to Christian values. The thought of the priesthood often entered his mind. Meanwhile his father was busy trying to arrange a good marriage for him. Unable to convince his father that he had no inclination to the married state, he finally had recourse to the somewhat comic retort that a man with such terrible asthma was not fitted for the joys of spousal love!

Still Alphonsus hesitated about the priesthood. An incredibly humiliating frustration did the trick. He had been working on a complicated legal case. With a reputation for winning the most difficult of these battles, he was flabbergasted when he lost this one because of a minor mistake. In a fit of pique, he decided to give up law altogether. He took his frustration in law as a sign that God wanted him to be a priest.

Of course, his ambitious father reviled him for thinking of giving up so prestigious a career after just one error. In response, Alphonsus, like St. Francis of Assisi before him, proclaimed, "I have no father but God."[2]

After quite a time of refusing to allow his son to study for the priesthood, the always ambitious father decided that if he could not budge his stubborn Alphonsus, at least he could arrange for him to pursue his vocation at home. At all costs he wanted to defeat the dream his son had of becoming a humble priest of the poor. Instead, he should emulate the type of bishop who managed to mingle an outward show of religiosity with wealth and power. By studying for the priesthood at home rather than at the seminary, Alphonsus could start on the fast track as we say today.

This plan of his father naturally frustrated Alphonsus who yearned to work as a priest for the poor. It is hard for twentieth-century readers to imagine how great a role parents played in the lives of their grown children in the past. To act without parental blessing was considered to be an outrage, worthy of God's punishment.

Desolate at the prospect of the compromises of being a priest in the image of the world, Alphonsus went into a church to beg God for guidance. The interior of the church became flooded with supernatural light. Under the power of this grace, Alphonsus was able to promise to become a priest without conditions, so eager was he to win souls instead of cases.

As a priest Alphonsus preached in the churches of Naples, as was to be expected, but he also taught poor children and prisoners. Soon he was surrounded by converted thieves, murderers, and prostitutes. Even his fierce father, who had blocked him every step on the way, had to accept him. The story is delightful. A storm forced the proud father to seek refuge in a church. There he heard his son preaching to the poor. He was amazed at the burning truth of the words of Alphonsus. History does not record the healing this must have been to the son after so many years of ridicule.

The father was not completely converted, however. It still rankled him that he could not take pride in having a rich prelate in the family. Instead his brainy son was to be holed up in the mountains giving retreats to abandoned village people. Alphonsus would live to see the day when his retreats became so popular that even nobility rode many miles to the tiny town where his monastery was located. His aging father came also, proud at last that everyone called his son a saint. He even wanted to stay in the poor monastery to do penance for his sins. Alphonsus deflected what was probably an enthusiastic whim by advising his father to return to the city to help his mother.

We now turn to the frustrations of Alphonsus that revolved around the founding of what would be known as the Redemptorist Order.

Through the mystical prayer of a nun, Christ directed Alphonsus to found an order for sisters later to be called the

Redemptoristines and also an order for preachers to the poor. The call to found these orders was confirmed by Our Lady in a miraculous locution. His plan was to travel around in the most desolate mountainous regions to preach missions to the poor with the prayerful support of the nuns.

This holy purpose was dogged by frustrations. In time, the nun with the founding mystical call left the order over a controversy. Naturally people interpreted this scandal as invalidating the original vision. After many years she would return repentant.

More seriously, most of the other priests who joined him in dedication to imitate the Redeemer by working among the poorest could not agree on the rule. Those who disagreed with Alphonsus about the plan for the order went to the cardinals and bishops and claimed that their founder was insane!

Faced with this frustration, coming not from men like his father who did not understand his values but from good zealous men who had loved him, Alphonsus fell into despair. He came against the misery invading his spirit by means of prayer and penance, finally deciding to take up the work alone if necessary,[3] hoping that eventually others would join him.

For a time he had to return in failure to preach in the city of Naples until he would be given permission to go back to the mountain villages he felt so called to evangelize.

The frustration of Alphonsus was alleviated when, attracted by his holiness, more and more priests decided to join him in the mission to the poor of the countryside. Trudging through mountain paths from village to village, Alphonsus became aware of the great ignorance of the people. He began to give retreats during this ministry and also to write hundreds of pamphlets, a practice that was to be an abiding part of the mission of the Redemptorist Order. Some of you may be familiar with Liguorian Magazine and the many booklets and books published by Redemptorist priests in the United States.

To try to become more holy himself, our Italian saint went in for the fierce bodily penances, so characteristic of saints of all times. In self-examination he would berate himself for overseriousness, impulsiveness, and bad temper. I found it interesting that he would put overseriousness in this list of flaws. In fact, many angry people given to experience frustration as intolerable are advised to relax more and especially to view life with greater humor.

Overseriousness comes from imagining it is I who am redeeming the world, a task that can never meet with anything but frustration! We can be lighter when we are convinced we are but faulty instruments in the hands of a Redeemer who is the main cause of any success that could result from our efforts.

Later, in trying to get his order approved by the king, a necessity in those days, he was continually frustrated by the delays imposed by royal ministers. Promised a quick response, he would be kept waiting days, weeks, years!

There is a humorous description of Alphonsus in his usual ragged garments waiting in the courtyard of the palace to see the king with his petition. The guard told Alphonsus to keep his head down as he left; his royal highness' hobby of shooting birds out in the piazza resulted in his often hitting the visitors instead!

The response of the saint to such outrageous frustrations was to pray and to keep on with his missions. He would have to wait for many decades to come for the full approval of his beloved order.

He tried to overcome his anger at the constant postponement of this needed official approval by intense work in travelling through the mountains to reach the poor and ignorant and in writing. During this time he was gifted with locutions, trances, levitations, bilocations. When Alphonsus came to give a mission in a town, the whole village would close down for lack of business. So powerful were the graces poured out that the prostitutes of the region would repent and become nuns.

Such sanctity could not be hid under a bushel basket. Soon the hierarchy of the church were pressuring him to become a bishop. He resisted many times but finally he was forced under obedience to comply. To deal with the frustration entailed by city life far from the abandoned life of the country, he reformed the usual lifestyle of a bishop by bringing in missions to the parishes, helping the poor, confessing lapsed Catholics and himself going door to door on his donkey to evangelize. He used all the funds others bishops would have spent for luxuries to buy food for the needy. At seventy-two, our zealous saint was still writing and still traveling by donkey.

One would think that God would take pity on this tired servant and take him away to heaven. But, no. At this time the life of Alphonsus became even more frustrating! Paralyzed, he was forced to lie in bed all day. As soon as he had recovered enough to celebrate Mass, he arranged for two seminarians to hold him up on either side so that he could make the consecration. What a model for priests of our time who sometimes think it unnecessary to celebrate Mass during the week if another priest is available.

Having written pamphlets, he now had time to write more and more large books. As a doctor of the church, he is most famous for his texts on moral theology, especially designed to help priests overcome the false alternative of harshness or of laxity in favor of a firmness that would not lack mercy. He is also loved for books still enjoying a huge circulation today about the glories of Mary and of the Eucharist.[3]

Possibly those who read his books, without benefit of having studied his life, picture him writing them at a beautiful desk in the calm and peace of a European library. If so, the real-life story in the next few paragraphs will add to your joy in seeing how a saint meets Christ even under the most horrible circumstances.

Our biographer next shows us Alphonsus even older and

more disabled. The younger, more ambitious members of his community are trying to change their way of life contrary to the discernments of Alphonsus.[4] Naturally, as the leader of the order, he desperately wants to address a meeting of the brethren to defend his point of view. Unable to walk or to hear or see well, he prays and prays for strength to be able to get to the room where the wrong decisions are being made. What frustration as the old saint tries to walk and falls into a heap sobbing.

To his despair the brothers got him to agree to altering the rule by having him sign a writ when he was too blind to read it, assuring him that it was just as he had wanted.[5] When they saw how angry this made him, they even voted him out of the order!

After a long time of struggle and with great anguish, Alphonsus forgave his brothers publically saying just before his Mass: "I wish only what God wishes. His grace is sufficient."[6]

To bring himself to forgive, he identified with Christ, saying that it was not enough to accept the cross but one must carry it as Christ did, among mocking faces, spat upon.[7]

As all angry people know, forgiveness does not take place completely in one great act. After his offering of forgiveness in humble resignation, Alphonsus was tempted to despair, the devil telling him that God hated him. So terrible was his misery that he pounded his forehead and dug his nails into his cheeks. For six years he lived on in disability but finally was reconciled with all his enemies in the order. Many brothers left during this confusing time. Alphonsus went through a year of blaming himself for all the problems of the order, battling with such scruples that he thought he was going mad.

Here are some of the words of Alphonsus himself about frustration and anger taken from *The Sermons of St. Alphonsus Liguori*.[8] The saint is commenting on the text, "Whosoever is angry with his brother, shall be in danger of the judgment" (Mt 22) and other related Scriptural passages.

Anger resembles fire; hence, as fire is vehement in its action, and, by the smoke which it produces, obstructs the view, so anger makes men rush into a thousand excesses, and prevents them from seeing the sinfulness of their conduct; and thus exposes them to the danger of the judgment of eternal death....

Anger is so pernicious to man, that it even disfigures his countenance. No matter how comely and gentle he may be, he shall, as often as he yields to the passion of anger, appear to be a monster and a wild beast full of terror....

But, if anger disfigures us before men, how much more deformed will it render us in the eyes of God!... Anger precipitates men into resentments, blasphemies, acts of injustice, detractions, scandals, and other iniquities; for the passion of anger darkens the understanding and makes a man act like a beast and a madman.... A man who does not restrain the impulse of anger, easily falls into hatred towards the person who has been the occasion of his passion....

In response to the rhetorical question about necessary anger of those in authority, Liguori says:

To be angry against sin is not anger but zeal; and therefore it is not only lawful but it is sometimes a duty. But our anger must be accompanied with prudence and must appear to be directed against sin, but not against the sinner; for if the person whom we correct perceives that we speak through passion and hatred towards him, the correction will be unprofitable.... Augustine says we are not allowed to hate others for their vices.

One might argue that God will take pity on us if we feel vengeful when we are unjustly dealt with. To this Liguori replies:

Who, I ask, has told you that you have just grounds for seeking revenge? It is you, whose understanding is clouded by passions, that say so... anger obscures the mind and takes away our reason and understanding. As long as the passion of anger lasts, you will consider your neighbor's conduct very unjust and intolerable; but when your anger shall have passed away, you shall see that his act was not so bad as it appeared to you.

But though the injury be grievous... God will not have compassion on you, if you seek revenge. No; he says: vengeance for sins belongs not to you but to me; and when the time shall come, I will chastise them as they deserve (see Deut 32:35).... If you resent an injury done to you... God will justly inflict vengeance on you for all the injuries you have offered to him, and particularly for taking revenge on a brother whom he commands you to pardon.... How can he who will not obey the command of God to pardon his neighbor expect to obtain from God the forgiveness of his own sins...

All the days of their life, persons addicted to anger are unhappy because they are always in a tempest.

How we ought to restrain anger in the occasions of provocation which occur to us:

In the first place, it is necessary to know that it is not possible for human weakness, in the midst of so many occasions, to be altogether free from every motion of anger.... All our efforts must be directed to the moderation of the feelings of anger which spring up in the soul.

How are they to be moderated? By meekness. This is called the virtue of the lamb—that is, the beloved virtue of Jesus Christ. Because, like a lamb, without anger or even complaint, he bore the sorrows of his passion and crucifixion... "Learn of me, because I am meek and humble of heart" (Mt 11:29)....

"Blessed are the peacemakers; for they shall be called the children of God".... You wish others to bear with your defects, and to pardon your faults; you should act in the same manner towards them. Whenever, then, you receive an insult from a person enraged against you, remember that "a mild answer breaketh wrath" (Prv 15:l).

The proud makes use of the humiliations they receive to increase their pride; but the humble and the meek turn the contempt and insults offered them into an occasion of advancing in humility. "He," says St. Bernard, "is humble, who converts humiliation into humility."

We must not become too frustrated with ourselves but deal with ourselves meekly.

When a person commits a fault, God certainly wishes him to humble himself, to be sorry for his sin, and to purpose never to fall into it again; but he does not wish him to be indignant with himself and give way to trouble and agitation of mind; for while the soul is agitated, a man is incapable of doing good.

As long, then, as anger lasts, we must be silent, and abstain from doing or resolving to do anything; for what is done in the heat of passion will, according to the maxim of St. James, be unjust. "The anger of man worketh not the justice of God" (Jas 1:20).[9]

Such are the teachings of a saint much tried, as we have shown, in the miseries of frustration and the temptation to anger.

Alphonsus Liguori died in his nineties having written one hundred books. He was beatified in 1816, canonized in 1839, and declared a Doctor of the Church in 1871. The true rule he had fought for was approved four years after his death. The order continuing his work in Portugal, Belgium, Holland and the United States, is supported in contemplative prayer by the Redemptoristine Sisters.

Are there any other saints who have gone through frustration and can share their wisdom with us? Some short and some longer stories of their struggles and their insights follow.

From the early church we have these incisive thoughts:[10]

Anger is a kind of temporary madness. **St. Basil**

Tell me, how are we... going to face the Day of Judgment? The sun is witness that has gone down on our anger not one day but for many a long year... **St. Jerome**

If a man cannot bear being reviled, he will not see glory. If he is not cleansed of gall, he will not savor sweetness.

St. Barsanuphius

St. Bernard of the twelfth century, like so many of the saints, was extremely bold and creative in the face of frustration.[11] He had left his beloved monastic solitude to help restore the true papacy. In this goal he was blocked by a certain Duke of Aquitaine who was an extremely powerful and evil man.

Bernard met with the Duke and seemed to win him over by his renowned persuasive powers, but later this Duke became even more ferocious and disobedient. In an unprecedented dramatic move, Bernard began the celebration of a Mass, then laid the sacred host on the paten, left the altar and moved toward the Duke, telling him with eyes flashing that he was guilty of despising Christ by despising his servants. The terrified Duke fell to the ground. Bernard insisted he be reconciled to the true pope before returning to the Mass. He did so and later left all his riches and power to become a penitent.[11]

When it seemed that all his efforts to save the real pope from the forces of the anti-pope might fail due to political machinations, Bernard would shuttle back and forth between countries always appealing to the better nature of the people he sought to reconcile. Bernard's belief that those in opposition to him did have a better nature is a good model for us of how to proceed in our own battles without the usual bitterness and calumny which so often comes with frustration.

To turn to still another example of St. Bernard's response to frustration, when some royal person he was directing took wrong turns politically, Bernard upbraided him. He threatened him with God's punishment and told him to accept this reprimand because "the wounds of a friend are better than the kisses of an enemy."[12] He employed much patient perseverance in bringing about political reconciliations.

Very often St. Bernard would take someone aside who opposed him and speak to him heart to heart with fine results, but if that didn't work he would rebuke someone directly from the pulpit, reminding him of the day of judgment.[13]

Many times in the lives of the saints we see frustration of their original dreams leading to the true vocation. Think of how much Francis of Assisi wanted to be a knight. Returning sick, he had ample time to respond to the real plan of God.

St. Catherine of Siena, the fiery Italian saint so noted for her own sweetness, wrote: "There is no sin nor wrong that gives a man such a foretaste of hell in this life as anger and impatience. O lovely compassion. You are the balm that snuffs out rage and cruelty in the soul. This compassion, compassionate Father, I beg you to give to all."[14]

St. Teresa of Avila, who endured many irritations and frustrations in her attempts to found reformed convents says that we should try to work on possible things versus dreaming about things that are truly impossible.[15]

Teresa was often frustrated when the slowness of the mail— in those days it could take many months for letters to arrive—

would increase the misunderstandings. In cases of rancor due to failure to understand the real motives behind her actions, she would double her loving attentions to those who were upset with her.[16] Yet she always maintained her convictions.

In general, St. Teresa believed that frustrations come when one acts unseasonably: "...we must trust in God's providence and one day it will be revealed."[17]

As to the frustration of feeling hemmed in by having too many people in a small space, St. John of the Cross advised going for solitary walks, sometimes taking all the brothers of a monastery for outings.[18]

St. John Vianney, the much persecuted nineteenth-century parish priest of Ars, France, taught that "The way to overcome the devil when he excites feelings of hatred for those who injure us is immediately to pray for their conversion."[19]

Let us end with a quotation from Venerable Jose Escriva noted for his sense of humor, to bring that light touch irascible people need so much: "Why lose your temper if by doing so you offend God, annoy other people, give yourself a bad time ... and have to find it again in the end."[20]

STEPS TO MEETING FRUSTRATIONS IN A CHRISTIAN SPIRIT

1. Never give up. Instead wait for the timing of God's providence. Notice that when the father of Alphonsus tried to block his projects, Alphonsus might agree to some nonessential element such as how to study, but he would refuse to give up on the main goal. When forced to be a bishop, he refused to give up his poor way of life and conducted his life as a bishop just the way he did as a Redemptorist—going door to door, and so on. Where

another man would have succumbed to illness, he cele-
brated Mass by having two seminarians hold him up.

2. Expect victory from God's grace rather than from your
    own schemes. Generally, angry people like to try to remove
    frustrations by force or cunning. But let us look at the
    model of St. Alphonsus. Could Alphonsus have manipu-
    lated such a father into affirming him? No, but God pro-
    vided a storm to bring him to the church where his son was
    preaching. Alphonsus did not beg his father to come to a
    retreat. He was drawn by the admiration for his son of his
    rich friends.

3. If others who should be allies block you, do everything
    alone until God sends you the right comrades. Often in
    such circumstances we quit, but if something is God's will
    we should keep on regardless of seeming defeat.

4. When discouraged, devote more time to prayer and
    penance.

5. When there seems to be no more hope at all, accept the
    frustration as God's permissive will and forgive your ene-
    mies, hoping for victory after death.

SIX

Meeting Christ in the Suffering of Interior Trials

Why art you cast down, O my soul, and why are you dis-quieted within me? Hope in God; for I shall again praise him, my help and my God. Psalm 42:5-6

My God, my God, why hast thou forsaken me? Psalm 22:1

All pain has an interior component. Here we want to treat the type of pain that is almost totally inward and can attack the sufferer regardless of what is good and bad in outward situations. After describing how St. Catherine of Genoa met Christ amidst incredible interior trials, I will describe some discoveries from other saints about such states as boredom, aridity, intense yearning for God, remorse for imperfections of character and for sins, and finally the worst of interior trials: despair.

ST. CATHERINE OF GENOA AND INTERIOR TRIALS

Born in 1447 to a noble family in Genoa, Catherine was the youngest of five, brought up for a life of luxury.[1] Yet by the age of eight, she had begun a life of penance by sleeping on straw at night instead of remaining in her own bed. Extraordinarily gifted with supernatural graces, the quiet and obedient girl wanted to enter a convent. She asked permission of her parents when she was eighteen.

Not only did her parents refuse to entertain the idea of a vocation to the religious life, but they insisted instead on marrying her off to Giuliano Adorno, an older man, whose family belonged to an opposing political group. The purpose of the marriage was to try to bring the two factions to peace. We might say that it was the exact reverse of Romeo and Juliet, with all the desire on the side of the families and all the incompatibility on the side of the spouses.

The differences between the two did not only involve personal taste but also divergence of character, for Giuliano was a difficult, unpleasant man, imprudent to the point of bankrupting the family. By contrast, Catherine was passionate, loving and dedicated. Her portrait shows her to have been tall, handsome with a delicately refined face, and a tender expression of love. Catherine later came to consider the unhappiness of her marriage as a gift of God, leaving her free from inordinate love of creatures for devotion to her true spouse, Jesus Christ.[2]

The young wife sought refuge in the company of other women. But no amount of frivolous chatter, for which she would later berate herself, could compensate for the coldness of her marriage, really a sort of abandonment. This deprivation of love sank the young woman into a state of melancholic depression.

Now one of Catherine's sisters was a nun. Worried about the state of Catherine's soul, she urged her to go to confession to a holy priest.

She had hardly knelt down... when her heart was suddenly pierced by an immense love of God, with such a clear awareness of her own miseries and sins and of God's goodness, that she was ready to swoon. The feeling produced in her a change of heart that purified her and drew her wholly away from the follies of the world…. She cried out in her heart with burning love: "No more world! No more sin!… she returned home, all on fire… as if beside herself, she chose out the most private room there was and there gave vent to her burning tears and sighs. The only prayer she could think of to say was: "O Love, is it possible that you have called me with so much love and have revealed to me in one moment what no tongue can describe?"[3]

During the next few days she saw visions of Christ on the cross and her whole house seemed full of streams of blood, shed for the sins of the world. Often this vision took the form of the Sacred Heart of Jesus suffering for love of sinners.

Continuing her usual life as manager of household affairs, she would spend six hours a day in prayer, rapt in a trance of love. She loved Holy Communion to such a degree that she would experience physical pain if deprived of him for a day.[4]

For four years Catherine devoted herself to prayer, penance, and tending the most repulsive cases among the sick and dying. During this time her husband began to repent of his past attitudes. He agreed to live as brother and sister and devote himself with her to the ministry to the sick, living in a poor district near the hospital.

During the years of 1477 to 1499, Catherine continued the penance of fasting, but gave up severe flagellations. Her ecstatic life of contemplative union with God attracted followers. She died at sixty-three from cancer of the stomach and nervous disorders. She immediately became a most popular saint. I find it fascinating to ponder the special love the English converts of the nineteenth century had for this so flamboyantly expressive mystical woman.

There are wonderful joyful passages in the sayings of Catherine. Apparently, she was so overjoyed when she saw death approaching that she laughed merrily for delight in the vision of the faces of the saved. However, most of what we know of her life and visions indicate a depression and despair so overwhelming as to be frightening to those around her and even to readers at four centuries distance. Consider this passage:

> She would bite her hands and burn them and this in order to divert, if possible, her interior oppression.... The only person left with whom she found any relief was her confessor, but then he too was taken away from her, and it came to the point that there was nothing more he could say to her or do to help her. At times she would seem to have her mind in a mill and it were grinding her, soul and body. Then she would... retire alone into a room and throw herself on the ground crying, "Love, I cannot bear it any longer!" She would continue with great lamentation, writhing like a serpent, and her moans could be heard by all those in the house.[5]

Most of all, she felt isolated from the rest of humanity by the vividness of her interior life of contemplation of hell, purgatory, and heaven. She would implore the Lord: "What would you have me do further in this world? I neither see nor hear, nor eat nor sleep. I do not know what I do or what I say. I feel as though I were a dead thing. There is no creature that understands me. I find myself lonely, unknown, poor, naked, strange and different from the rest of the world."[6]

St. Catherine of Genoa believed that her feelings of despair and abandonment were part of being as close to Christ as she was. She would say that she could not bear any words about her relationship to God that indicated any distance between them such as love *for* God. Instead, she insisted that God was "my me," for love is God.[7]

Catherine taught that we must accept being annihilated in God just as a piece of bread is annihilated upon entering into us. Out of love it is a joy to suffer. Jesus once told her: "Observe these three rules. Never say 'I will,' or 'I will not.' Never say 'my' but always 'our.'"[8]

INTERIOR TRIALS OF TEDIUM AND BOREDOM

The title of this section might be puzzling to some readers. Active happy temperaments tend to regard tedious, boring times as little hurdles until the good things begin to happen again. Actually, sometimes overactivity comes from fear of the emptiness of boring times. Facing vacuity can be necessary to advance to a deeper level of action motivated more by God's will than by a need to fill time quickly.

For melancholy temperaments, tedium can be one of the most miserable of sufferings. It does not have the drama of real darkness, but is more like a grey pall on everything! In boredom, relationships and works that previously were exciting and challenging become dull as dishwater, and this tepid state of being can last not just for hours or days but for years on end.

Many people look upon tedium as simply a symptom of lack of exercise or a spoiled ingratitude for the good gifts of God. This may be true in some cases. But boredom can also have a spiritual cause. Listen to St. Teresa: "When the soul has learned through experience that creatures cannot give it true rest, everything wearies the soul."[9]

St. John of the Cross thought a remedy for tedium was variety. He used to take the novices for long walks in the country "so that when one is in the convent, one may have less desire to leave it."[10]

Our third renowned Carmelite saint, Thérèse of Lisieux wrote in her journal: "This evening I felt a need... to forget the earth. Here below everything wearies me, everything is an effort. I find only one joy, to suffer for Jesus...." She suggests overcoming this weariness by fixing our minds on eternal life, on the new heavens, on the immensity of our abode in heaven where we will no more be prisoners in this exile. "With our heavenly spouse, we shall skim over lakes with no shore..."[11]

INTERIOR TRIALS OF ARIDITY

Some Christians have never really heard of aridity, though many experience it perpetually. Called the desert in some books of spiritual guidance, it is basically a period of extreme dryness in prayer, often following a time of joyful sensing of God's presence and love.

It can impress the believer as a sort of rejection, just as in marriage some wives and husbands feel deeply grieved when a frothily happy honeymoon is followed by a more humdrum time of uneventful daily life.

Doctors of the Church who write about God's ways with his friends would be more likely to see aridity not as a proof of rejection but as a fulfillment of these words of Jesus: "Blessed are the poor in Spirit, for theirs is the kingdom of heaven" (Mt 5:3).

The purpose of an arid phase in a spiritual journey is not to quench the spirit but to purify the soul of any gluttonous desire for constant excitement, so that a tranquil union can abide amidst the ups and downs of life, similar to the relatively peaceful union of an old, happily married couple.

Concerning the anxiety caused by aridity, St. Teresa wrote: "There is no need for us to be advising him about what he should give us, for he can rightly tell us that we don't know what we are asking for. Do God's will and he shall give you more."[12]

It is said of St. Jane of Chantal that she experienced the longest period of aridity of any saint on the calendar. Here is how she met her beloved Christ in the midst of her desert: "Today again, more or less, there remains very little for me to rest upon and so repose my spirit; perhaps this good Lord wishes to put his holy hand in all the places of my heart so as to take everything from it and despoil it of all. May his holy will be done!"[13]

Thérèse of Lisieux, also much subject to this interior trial, used to say that she preferred sacrifice to ecstasy.[14] She thought of aridity as an interior martyrdom known to God alone, without honor, therefore very heroic, a choice offering of love.

Thérèse said that she wished to be with the Lord in prayer not to be comforted but to comfort him. She didn't even mind if she slept during her prayer time, thinking of how children are dear to their parents especially asleep![15]

Feeling arid, Thérèse would invite into her soul all the angels and saints so that they could receive Jesus since she was so dry. When bored by prayers such as the rosary, she would focus on her intention of love, or she would pray slowly and this would take her out of herself better than muttering them fast. Thérèse wrote that she preferred the Scriptures and the *Imitation of Christ* to other spiritual reading.

How much like most of us she sounds when she says:

Life is often a burden; such bitterness, but such sweetness!... If only one felt Jesus close at hand! Oh! One would do all for him... but no, he seems a thousand leagues away, we are alone with ourselves.... But what can that loving friend be doing? Doesn't he see our anguish, the weight that is crushing us? Where is he, why does he not come to console us, since we have no friend but him?... He is not far off, he is here, close, looking at us, begging us to offer him this grief, this agony.... He needs it for souls, for our soul. He means to give us so splendid a reward.... it is great pain to him thus to fill our cup with sorrows, but he knows that is the only way to prepare us 'to know him as he knows himself'... Jesus is hidden but one senses him....[16]

THE INTERIOR TRIAL OF INTENSE YEARNING FOR GOD

In a way, this torment is the exact opposite of the aridity we have just been describing, yet it is also characteristic of the life of all ardent Christians. We feel its presence in the beloved Psalm 42:

As a hart longs for flowing streams,
    so longs my soul for thee, O God.
My soul thirsts for God,
    for the living God.
When shall I come and behold the face of God?

In *The Life of Mary as Seen by the Mystics*, Raphael Brown describes the great yearning of Mary as a young girl for the coming of the Messiah. The love of God burned in her heart with ever new fervor and longing.[17] The visionaries also tell of Mary's great yearning to be with Jesus after his ascension.

When the soul arrives at the seventh mansion of the Interior Castle in St. Teresa's classic, it is the yearning for God that becomes the greatest interior trial.[18] Seeing death as the only way to come to fulfillment of their great love for God, they long for it with intense yearning.

In his ecstatic supernatural love poetry, John of the Cross brings out the pain of the soul touched by love but not yet fulfilled:

Where have you hidden,
Beloved, and left me moaning?
You fled like the stag
After wounding me;
I went out calling you, and you were gone...

Ah, who has the power to heal me?
Now wholly surrender yourself!
Do not send me
Any more messengers,
They cannot tell me what I must hear.

All who are free
Tell me a thousand graceful things of you;
All wound me more
And leave me dying
Of, ah, I-don't-know-what behind their stammering.

How do you endure
O life, not living where you live?
And being brought near death
By the arrows you receive
From that which you conceive of your beloved.

Why, since you wounded
This heart, don't you heal it?
And why, since you stole it from me,
Do you leave it so,
And fail to carry off what you have stolen?[19]

INTERIOR TRIALS OF SCRUPLES AND REMORSE FOR FAULTS OF CHARACTER AND FOR SINS

Given the radiant goodness of God and the graces he pours out on us through his Son's redemption and through the sanctification of the Holy Spirit, is it not natural that sinful humanity should feel much pain at the thought of our betrayal of so loving a God?

Yes. Contrition is a painful but beautiful response to the real-

ity of our sin and God's mercy. This emotion is enshrined forever in Psalm 51:

Have mercy on me, O God,
according to thy steadfast love;
according to thy abundant mercy
blot out my transgressions.
Wash me thoroughly from my iniquity,
and cleanse me from my sin!
For I know my transgressions,
and my sin is ever before me.
Against thee, thee only, have I sinned,
and done that which is evil in thy sight,
so that thou are justified in thy sentence and blameless in thy
      judgment....
Behold, thou desirest truth
in the inward being;
therefore teach me wisdom
in my secret heart.
Purge me with hyssop,
and I shall be clean;
wash me, and I shall be whiter than snow.
Fill me with joy and gladness;
let the bones which thou hast broken rejoice.
Hide thy face from my sins,
and blot out all my iniquities.
Create in me a clean heart, O God,
and put a new and right spirit within me.
Cast me not away from thy presence,
and take not thy holy Spirit from me.
Restore to me the joy of thy salvation,
and uphold me with a willing spirit...
The sacrifice acceptable to God is a broken spirit;
a broken and contrite heart,
O God, thou wilt not despise.

The psalmist beautifully depicts the mixture of pain and joy that accompanies true contrition: sorrow for sin, but delight in God's merciful love.

Quite another kind of suffering is that of scruples and despairing remorse. The scrupulous Christian is one who exaggerates guilt by blaming himself or herself too much for movements of imperfection and evil outside the range of free will. Feeling ourselves to be sinks of iniquity, we give ourselves no credit whatsoever for our struggles against evil, imagining that even to have bad thoughts or to fall suddenly when we are off guard into venial sins already merits hellfire.

In the attitude of remorse, instead of trusting in God's cleansing mercy, expressed in the sacrament of reconciliation, the sinner considers himself or herself to be damned for real past sins. An example in our day would be women and men involved in abortion, unable to believe that God can forgive them, no matter how often they confess the past sin or make atonement through pro-life witness.

Remorse that does not lead to the hope that follows contrition can become an attitude of self-blame which says I can never forgive myself even if God forgives me. This feeling, though seemingly humble, is really proud, for it implies that one has fallen from a great height rather than admitting that we are so weak that we will always fall unless God saves us. It denies that all things are possible with God, including my own reformation in grace.

This attempt at a clear intellectual analysis of scrupulosity and bitter remorse, gives no accurate picture of the interior sufferings of those who afflict themselves in these distorted ways. It will be helpful to describe even a few saints who went through long periods of these trials, certainly at least in giving hope that they need not be permanent states of mind.

We need not to mull over our sins in impotent remorse, but instead to meet Christ in our sorrow for sin, realizing that if he willed to die for our sins, we owe him trust in his mercy.

This famous prayer of Saint Gertrude the Great of the thirteenth century is a good one for those afflicted with painful scruples or remorse:

> *O most loving Father,*
> *in atonement and satisfaction for all my sins*
> *I offer thee the whole passion of thy most beloved Son,*
> *from the plaintive wail he uttered*
> *when laid upon the straw in the manger,*
> *through all the helplessness of his infancy,*
> *the privations of his boyhood,*
> *the adversities of his youth,*
> *the sufferings of his manhood,*
> *until that hour when he bowed his head upon the cross*
> *and with a loud cry gave up his Spirit.*
> *And in atonement and satisfaction*
> *for all my negligences,*
> *I offer thee, O most loving Father*
> *the most holy life and conversations of thy Son,*
> *most perfect in his every thought, word, and action,*
> *from the hour when he came down*
> *from his lofty throne*
> *to the Virgin's womb,*
> *and thence came forth into our dreary wilderness,*
> *to the hour*
> *when he presented to thy fatherly regard*
> *the glory of his conquering flesh. Amen.*

(From a prayer card)

It might be helpful to know that one of the most level-headed of saints had problems with scrupulosity. After his conversion Ignatius Loyola constantly asked himself whether his confessions where complete. Unsure, he would fall into despair and temptation to suicide, imagining a happy end to his torment if he would throw himself into an abyss. In his prayer he tempted God by deciding to fast completely until God would give him peace of soul. The confessor of Ignatius made him stop fasting. Still the scrupulous Ignatius felt despair, but then suddenly experienced a rebirth. This was followed by tremendous visions of the Trinity[20] which greatly fortified him. Later on, he would become an excellent counselor for driving away scruples from others.

Many Christians wonder why God allows them to fall into sin in the first place, since they are trying so hard. In scrupulosity, they come to believe that they are especially evil so that no amount of grace can help them. The practical wisdom and advice of St. Teresa of Avila, who considered herself to have been a great sinner, is very helpful: "Sometimes he even permits these reptiles (sins) to bite us so that afterwards we can know how to guard ourselves better and that he may prove whether we are greatly grieved by having offended him."[21]

Teresa believed that scruples can be increased by unintelligent confessors. Scrupulous persons should avoid too much solitude and concentrate on good works.[22]

It should always be remembered, Teresa taught, that some saints who fell into serious sins "had greater happiness and closeness to God than others who did not."[23] Humorously, she relates how her nuns like to think she had led a holy life but that really she had sinned much and relied on mercy alone.

The remedy of frequent confession for scruples and exaggerated remorse was much recommended by such saints as John of the Cross,[24] John Vianney, and Cardinal Newman.

St. Thomas More, the brilliant future Lord Chancellor of England, during a period in his life when he seemed to be failing in everything, became subject to an alarming fear of hell. He thought that he had been so proud as a youth that God had sent him failure to break him and as a foretaste of the hell he was destined for.[25] He would lie awake for hours fearing eternal punishment. His Carthusian confessor advised him to allay his fears by following Christ more closely and by trusting in mercy and in his confessor, just as he expected his clients coming to him for legal advice to trust him.

The fears lasted a long time and abated only through immersion in hard work: legal toil chosen above his beloved literary work, done out of charity for his own family who needed the income. After this period he felt great joy.

Blessed Marie of the Incarnation, the Ursuline missionary nun who helped evangelize Canada in the seventeenth century had four years of intense suffering due to scrupulosity.[26] Her sufferings came from feeling so ashamed of not being able to overcome her resentments of others involved in her ministry. She wanted to feel only love but had to admit to:

> ... a bitterness aimed at some good and holy people... whenever anything arises capable of stirring antipathy this the most painful thing in the world for a soul who fears God and sin and who loves purity of heart.... The soul is desperately afraid of being deluded... it believes it has never had any solid virtue. Whatever it thought to have received interiorly it now feels has not come from God.[27]

She attributes these painful feelings of remorse to the work of God purifying the soul by causing such misery whenever we slip into some sort of compromise spirit, trying to blend together somehow one's natural flaws with the purity of God's grace. God allows us to be humiliated so that our vanity would be mortified, and we might eventually long only for God's grace in total annihilation of our own passions.[28]

About this state of suffering she would later write to a Jesuit priest:

Yet God makes all this (her faults) compatible with a state of union which has kept me bound to his Divine Majesty for several years without deviating from it a single moment.... During this period God shines at the depth of the soul, which is, as it were, in waiting, like a person whom one interrupts while he is speaking to another and who, nevertheless, still maintains the sight of the person to whom he is talking. The soul, as it were, waits in silence before returning to its intimate union.... The effects of this state are peace of heart in temporal events and the desire to want only what God wants in all the effects of his divine providence as they occur from moment to moment.[29]

Do you still remember St. Benedict Labre of our chapter on failure? The wretched boy longed to become a Trappist monk against the will of his parents and also of the abbots of the monasteries he tried to enter. Twice he was admitted and both times he fell into unbearable scrupulosity, especially about unworthy reception of Holy Communion. So far did this go that it led into a darkness that threatened his sanity.[30] Since he was free of this degree of mental anguish outside of the monastery, his experience seems to show that for some a change of scene to a much more low-pressure environment can be a help.

About pain of remorse, St. Thérèse of Lisieux told her sister Celine: "Do not try to rise above your trials, for we are too small to rise above our difficulties. Therefore let us try to pass under them.... If you bear in peace the trial of being displeasing to yourself, you offer a sweet shelter to Jesus. It is true that it hurts you to find yourself thrust outside the door of your own self, so to speak, but fear not; the poorer you become, the more Jesus will love you."[31]

Now is a good time to ponder the quotation from the novelist Paul Scott: "We must remember the worst because the worst is the lives we lead, the best is only our history, and between our history and our lives there is this vast dark plain where the rapt and patient shepherds drive through invisible flocks in expectation of God's forgiveness."[32]

And surely an example of such a rapt and patient shepherd was Venerable Jose Escriva who wrote about scruples: "Love Our Lady. And she will obtain abundant grace for you to help you conquer in your daily struggle. And the enemy will gain nothing by those foul things that continually boil and rise within you, seeking to swallow up in their perfumed corruption the high ideals, the sublime determination that Christ Himself has set in your heart."[33]

THE INTERIOR TRIALS OF DEPRESSION AND DESPAIR

In this section of the chapter, I am linking together depression and despair, not because they are really the same, but because one of the worst parts of depression is the fear of sliding into despair. What is the difference? In depression we feel very, very sad and imagine that we will never feel better until heaven, but there is hope of heaven. In despair all hope seems to disappear and we feel as abandoned by God, if he exists, as did Jesus crying out from the cross, "My God, my God, why have you abandoned me."

Psychologists tell us depression and despair can be the result of chemical imbalance. They certainly can come from mental imbalance of such conditions as the manic-depressive or psychotic. And these states of mind can easily lead to suicidal tendencies. What relationship exists between the physical, the psychological, and the spiritual in such terrible levels of consciousness is not altogether clear. Spiritual directors trying to help those in depression and despair will usually seek medical and psychological help to supplement their own insights.

I would not want what is written here about depression and despair, viewed from the standpoint of stages of holiness, to lead any reader to postpone medical or psychological help on the grounds that all you need is trust in God.

On the other hand, within the stages of the dark nights delineated so carefully by St. John of the Cross, a sufferer may take hope in the knowledge that troubles which seem unique to oneself and without any possible improvement, are truly necessary steps toward holiness.

Read this description from the Spanish Doctor of the Church to see:

> This night is a painful disturbance involving many fears, imaginings, and struggles within a man. Due to the apprehension and feeling of his miseries, he suspects that he is lost and that his blessings are gone forever. The sorrow and moaning of his spirit is so deep that it turns into vehement spiritual roars and clamorings... indescribable spiritual anguish and suffering.
>
> These are the effects produced in the soul by this night which enshrouds the hopes one has for the light of day....: This war or combat is profound because the peace awaiting the soul must be exceedingly profound; and the spiritual suffering is intimate and penetrating because the love to be possessed by the soul will also be intimate and refined....[34]

St. John of the Cross will go on to explain that the darkness is like fire burning wood. The old log that is almost burned is very ugly, but the effect is the beautiful light of the fire. So our souls feel dark and ugly as Christ is purifying them. After the dark night of the soul is over, we will be light and beautiful.

As a Carmelite contemplative nun of our times writes about deep interior suffering:

There is a place in the heart where pain and joy meet, where pain is ecstatic, while still being pain.... We have a choice to go forward or go back. When the pain reaches an almost unbearable degree (whatever its cause), we must decide to go with the pain or go back (though the going back really does not decrease the pain). If we go with the pain, we enter a place in the heart that opens into the heart of God and there the pain is changed.

Even while it is felt as excruciating, it is also a soothing balm, a medicine that heals us and gives us joy, and we know that this is a place of love and that the pain is proof of love. And we meet God heart to heart. We plunge into the wounded heart of Jesus... we leave our wounded and pain-filled hearts and enter that place of refuge and divine delight, a furnace of love that consumes all shame and inflames us with deeper desire, but that too is delightful.... This is a most intimate meeting place with Jesus and those we love... it is the marriage bed, the place of spousal intimacy.

Anonymous

Christians experiencing depression and despair would do well to study *The Dark Night of the Soul* by St. John of the Cross carefully over a long period of time with the help of a spiritual director.

Blessed Marie of the Incarnation, mentioned already under the title of scruples, also had several long bouts with despair. Her whole story will be found in our chapter about loneliness. Here I only want to describe a particular time of despair. When Marie was a widow with a small son, she was graced with beautiful illuminative visions, taking place in the midst of a busy life helping with the family docking works. She would go into ecstacies while watering down the horses!

Receiving permission from her spiritual director to follow her longing to become a nun, at age thirty-one she entered the

Ursulines leaving her son to the care of the extended family.

After a few months of novitiate, darkness fell upon her soul.[35] She thought she was losing her mind. All her previous vivacious love for God seemed paralyzed. The editor of the book of her selected writings says of this period in her life that the darkness could be interpreted not only as the classical dark night of the soul but also as an experience that can come to many highly active Catholic women who dream of a more contemplative life but really need the outlet of activity to avoid depression.[36] In any case it would be alleviated when she was given a vision of a beautiful land where Jesus and Mary were waiting for her. The image was an exact picture of the part of Canada to which she would travel as a missionary. She realized that even though she had chosen the Ursuline monastery, her zeal for evangelizing unreached people was so great she could not be shut up in a convent.

Alphonsus Liguori, described in our chapter on frustration, went through terrible despair toward the end of his long life when almost everyone in the order had betrayed him. The devil came to tell him that all his life he had served a God who rewarded him with pain, blindness, and paralysis. Surely such a God was a God not of love but of hate. Alphonsus writhed in pain, pounding his forehead, digging his nails into his cheeks, begging all to pray for him. Then the despair lifted.

Of Venerable Francis Liebermann, whose life is described in detail in our chapter about fear, it is written:

At all times, the undercurrent of his soul was suffering—the suffering of loneliness, of failure, of nervous affliction that held out no hope. Discouragement sometimes overwhelmed him. Depression overpowered him and gave him no peace. It pursued him on the road to Issy and on the boulevards of Paris.

Most of all, when he crossed the Seine, it plagued him mercilessly. Those dark flowing waters possessed a strange attraction for him. Their siren-call floated up from under the majestic arches of the bridge: "Come, lose yourself in our embrace. Be done with this unbearable life for once and for all." At such times his muscles would grow taut as the temptation swept over him to scale the balustrade and let himself fall into the merciful river, ending this inhuman existence and ceasing at last to be a burden to himself and others.

In these black moments, the flame of faith seemed to die. He wanted to believe, he did believe, but it was all he could do to push his leaden feet ahead and hurry across the mesmerizing span. Once on the other side, he breathed normally again. The crisis had passed. But he subsequently confessed that he never crossed one of those bridges without feeling the diabolic urge to cast himself over the parapet into the waters below.[37]

He lived to be a saint because he always held onto Christ in the darkness, praying incessantly and refusing to give in to despair.

The French St. Thérèse said that when people were in great pain of sickness to be sure never to leave any medicines or potential poison near them for it was such a temptation to end it all by this handy means.[38]

STEPS IN MEETING CHRIST WHEN AFFLICTED WITH INTERIOR TRIALS

1. Cling to your confessor, spiritual director, and your closest friends for support during your trial. Make use also of any physical or psychological help that is available.

2. Never take for truth the negative thoughts that come to you during interior trials. Immerse yourself instead in Scripture and traditional prayers full of doctrinal truth.

3. Cast yourself into the arms of Christ even when you cannot see or feel his presence, begging for rescue.

4. During periods of anguish, study the lives of saints who have found Christ's love in the midst of similar sufferings and also read the Doctors of the Church who are experts on stages of interior pain on the road to holiness.

We now turn to the wisdom of the saints concerning particular trials, moving from least to worst.

SEVEN

Meeting Christ in the Suffering of Loneliness and Loss

Turn thou to me, and be gracious to me; for I am lonely and afflicted. Psalm 25:16

Behold, the dwelling of God is with men. He will dwell with them, and they shall be his people, and God himself will be with them; he will wipe away every tear from their eyes, and death shall be no more, neither shall there be mourning nor crying nor pain anymore, for the former things have passed away. Revelation 21:3-4

This is a chapter about the pain that comes with feeling isolated in loneliness or lonely for the presence of a loved one lost by death, separation, or rejection.

Since we are created to be one day part of the most perfect love union of all, the Holy Trinity, it is no wonder that loneliness feels so unnatural to us. Even one deprived of love in childhood will yearn for the closeness that has been denied, seeking for it sometimes through the momentary contact of sexual sin.

And then there is a loneliness that comes through loss, where we can compare a previous state of loving presence to a stark absence. And this has its own pain, different from the isolation of the loner, but also piercing, causing the anguish of grief.

Often the saints experienced a third type of loneliness in addition to isolation and loss. This was a closeness to God experienced as a separateness from others, even Christians. In reality, that which occupies the mind and heart of the saint every moment of the day is only a small part of the life of many believers, and these often regard the person not as a saint but as an absurd fanatic!

BLESSED MARIE OF THE INCARNATION: A LONELY PILGRIM

The year 1599 saw the birth of Marie Guyart in the French city of Tours.[1] She was the middle child in the family of a baker. She would live in the illustrious age of French spirituality led by such saints as de Sales, de Chantal, Eudes, Vincent de Paul, and Louise de Marillac.

At the age of seven, Marie had a supernatural dream. The Lord in resplendent beauty came toward her, embraced her with love, took her in his arms and kissed her, asking, "Will you be mine?" She answered, "Yes."[2]

During her youth she thought about a religious vocation, but her parents were against it. Already the motif of loneliness enters. Marie's parents did not understand the ardor of her religious nature but instead believed her character more suitable for marriage.

By eighteen Marie was married to Claude Martin, a merchant of the city. She had borne her first child but became at nineteen a widow. Now she was a single parent and also the "beneficiary" of a huge debt. Marie could have declared bankruptcy, but unexpectedly, she became convinced that if she put her mind to it, she could save the business.

Anyone in the world would think that the gift for business

the young woman displayed was but one more proof that she was meant for "normal" life, probably with another marriage in the offing. Evidently God had other wishes for her. In the midst of a typical day of hustle and bustle, Marie was suddenly caught up in a rapture. Accompanied by this invasion of the Holy Spirit came a profound and devastating realization of all the faults and sins she had committed during her whole life, together with a vision of the Precious Blood of Jesus being shed for her salvation.[3]

After this grace, Marie felt she had become a new person, full of love for Jesus the Redeemer. Ever after, Marie would live primarily not in the world but in union with God, especially oriented around devotion to the Sacred Heart, a passion for the Eucharist, and the immersion of her soul in the Holy Trinity. The high mystical gifts led swiftly toward the spiritual marriage of her soul with God at the age of twenty-seven. This climax of love altered Marie's interior life from longing and expectation to the possession of union.

From the human standpoint, it was a lonely "marriage" without the presence of any relatives or friends, for all those who surrounded her were business people whose main interests concerned monetary success.

To picture her loneliness, we have to go back to trace the more mundane side of Marie's life after the untimely death of her husband. As would be customary in those days, Marie lived in her parental home doing needlework to support her little child, her mother helping take care of the little boy.

Within a year she was asked to move to the house of her sister who needed Marie's help in the management of her household. It is easy for us in times where only the rich have live-in maids or nannies to think that the middle-class ladies of the house were elegant idlers. Reading biographies and novels of the time reveals quite a different life for the mistress of the house, one filled with frustrations and often recalcitrant servants. Besides, in the house of her sister lived not only the family and the servants but also the workman of her brother-in-law's carting business.

When Marie's sister's husband, Paul Buisson, became aware of how efficient his sister-in-law was, he induced her to become an assistant in his business. Now her work would take her to the docks to work with cursing stevedores, checking their loading work and making sure that invoices, merchandise, and cash were in order.

Although Marie hated this work, she did it so well that everyone was amazed when she wanted to enter the convent instead. She had only been able to bear the world because of the force of the love of Jesus in her heart, making its presence felt so strongly that nothing from outside could upset her.

Her biographer, Sister Irene Mahoney, points out that even if the dock work seemed antithetical to Marie's vocation, in fact it was a preparation for her later labors in the Canadian mission where she would need to understand the business dealings of the French colonists, adjusting herself to an atmosphere quite as crude and irreverent as the docks of France.[4]

Confidence in God's providence during this bleak time in Marie's outward circumstances would be a help also in the unbelievably difficult trials of the mission.

Reading about this period of our saint's life, I cannot help sensing the intense loneliness of it, for there is no indication that she found any echo of her own love for Christ in anyone in her immediate environment, save in the soul of her little son and in the advice of priestly directors.

At the age of thirty-one, she entered the Ursuline convent, attracted largely by their evangelical charism, devoted as they were to the salvation of souls, mainly through teaching. Perhaps she also imagined that she would find companionship in this order of other women who had consecrated themselves to the same Bridegroom.

But what was to become of her son, only eleven years old? This boy, who later was to become a priest, was most dear to his mother's heart. Although reserved in her affection, partly to prepare him for her future entrance into the cloister, her heart was pierced with suffering when the time came to fulfill a plan so supernaturally right but so humanly impossible.

After many years of struggle, Claude would come to understand the rightness of the decision which cast him into such loneliness in youth and young manhood. If God found a way to console the son, it does not seem to be our place, as onlookers, to try to judge the mother's decision.

Marie acted under obedience to her director and to what she judged to be mystical proofs of God's will that she become a consecrated woman. It is helpful to remember how much more bound together was the extended family of those times, and also how much more mature the youth.

Eleven would be about the time most boys of the middle and upper classes would be sent to boarding schools in any case. We must also remember that Marie's mystical union with God gave her so felt a sense of what heaven would be like, where she and her son would one day be enfolded in Christ's embrace, that she could steel herself to bear the temporary separation.

Nonetheless, the letters she wrote from Canada to her distant son, the person she was closest to in the whole world, make one's heart break for them both. A typical letter begins with these words:

> Your letter brought me so profound a consolation that it is very hard for me to describe it. All this year I have been in great torment, imagining the pitfalls where you might stumble. But finally our gracious God gave me peace in the belief that his loving and fatherly goodness would never lose what had been abandoned for his love....

You have been abandoned by your mother and your relatives, yet hasn't this abandonment been to your advantage?
When I left you before, you were twelve years old, I endured
terrible agonies of spirit which were known to God alone. I
had to obey his divine will... my heart was strengthened so
that I was able to overcome what had delayed my entry into
religious life for ten long years.... I foresaw that you would
be abandoned by your relatives, which cost me a thousand
pains; this, linked to human weakness, made me fear your
ruin.[5]

Marie constantly practiced abandonment to divine providence and surrender to his will in making decisions and in
accepting the pain that would follow. Peace would come when
praying before the Blessed Sacrament.

Our chapter about interior trials gives more detail about the
sufferings of Marie in the convent. At first she was delirious
with joy to be free of temporal concerns and able to devote herself only to the things of God, but within two months, there
came a terrible darkness with diabolical temptations, which
would only lift somewhat at the time of her profession. The veil
would lift still more through her vision two years afterwards of
a land full of forests and mountains, with Jesus and Mary greet-
ing her with open arms, a prophecy of the Canadian mission.[6]

It was during this period that the Jesuits were seeking dedicated Catholic women to join them in the missions in Canada.
Conditions at these sites have been graphically portrayed in a
recent film *Mission*. How important it could be to have women
to form the new converts of the Indian tribes. Where could they
find any courageous and hardy enough to risk so difficult an
undertaking? Who would be willing to forgo the safety of the
cloister for a vocation new to those times: the missionary sister?

Soon we find Marie and two other sisters in the company of
a laywoman, also a widow, Madeleine de la Peltrie, eager to

venture across the Atlantic (a three-month passage) to teach the faith to the pagans. In this way God's will would be done in extending his kingdom to the ends of the earth. With her sacrificial spirituality influenced by the Jesuits, all the hardships of the mission came as welcome penances. These included freezing cold, drastic poverty, brutal wars, and devastating fires.

Now comes another period of loneliness for Marie from a human standpoint. Her heart was filled by Christ's intimate love, and this would overflow in heroic charity toward the Indian children in her care. The problems lay in the other areas of mission life.

Externally, the Catholic mission women were isolated by the attitudes of many of the French colonists who exploited the Indians by bartering alcohol for native goods. These men had no concern for the newly baptized Indians. The formation of the Indians as Catholics was sabotaged by the hard liquor which produced unaccustomed effects that destroyed them more quickly than it did the French. Besides this, there were ferocious Indian wars with raiding parties burning missions.

From a more internal standpoint, Marie did not seem to find in the sisters and lay missionary the mutual love one would have expected. Goodness and forbearance, yes, but the easy, warm spiritual friendships of the type depicted by St. Bernard or St. Aelred, or of St. Francis de Sales and St. Jane, she didn't experience.

As described in the chapter on interior trials, Marie often engaged in long struggles with the ways and actions of the other missionary women. Always she would display charitable kindness, but internally she was filled with bitter antipathy.[7] After the worst difficulties of this kind, the sisters admitted to also having had an aversion to Marie.

So common are the petty and sometimes important reasons for disharmony in communities that there is no need to try to sift through to determine who was right. We only need to note here the desperate fidelity of Marie to her Bridegroom as she labored for the mission in so much loneliness, always combined with fear that her unloving feelings were a proof that she was a damned soul in spite of all her zeal.

In these fears Marie received much help from one of her confessors. She was also strengthened by making a vow to always do whatever was the most perfect thing she could choose for the glory of God.[8] Jesus himself would come to her in prayer with infinite tenderness. And finally, it was in praying to Mary that she obtained the grace to be lifted out of her state of aversion to the others surrounding her.[9]

After many trials Marie of the Incarnation was to end her solitary pilgrimage in her beloved mission territory of Canada in 1672 having laid down her life to bring her beloved Savior to the Indian people.

When we think of Mary and Joseph, we don't always think of their periods of loneliness and loss. Perhaps we like to imagine that they were so holy that knowing of the happy ending to their lives in the eventual victory of their son, they did not have to endure the human anguishes of loneliness or rejection or loss.

A little more reflection would give us a sense of the rejection from each other Mary and Joseph must have felt at the time of Joseph's uncertainty about their marriage. And what of the loneliness of setting out for Egypt with the infant Jesus pursued by Herod's soldiers? In spite of the closeness of their love for each other in the Holy Family, there is loneliness in an alien land far from the tight-knit families of their village.

What of the sense of loss when Jesus was missing in the temple, or the violent rejection when the men of Nazareth sought to throw Jesus off a cliff calling him insane and possessed? How could the horror of the crucifixion not be imbued also with a lonely feeling of being rejected by the people Jesus came to save, and even betrayed by those of the apostles who knew, but were afraid to follow.

Legend has it that Joseph died before the crucifixion so that Mary would have endured the loneliness of losing the one who best knew the real story of the graces of God filling her past and her hopes.

In spite of the loving companionship of St. John, how lonely was the Mother after her Son ascended into heaven.

All these sufferings would be offered by Mary, Joseph, and Jesus in reparation for the sins of their enemies and also for the sins of all humanity throughout the ages.

The Confessions of St. Augustine contains a most incisive approach to the miseries of the loss of loved ones in death.

During those years when I first began to teach in Thagaste, my native town, I had found a very dear friend. We were both the same age, both together in the heyday of youth, and both absorbed in the same interests. We had grown up together as boys, gone to school together, and played together.

Yet ours was not the friendship which should be between true friends, either when we were boys or at this later time. For though they cling together, no friends are true friends unless you, my God, bind them fast to one another through that love which is sown in our hearts by the Holy Ghost, who is given to us.

Yet there was sweetness in our friendship, mellowed by the interests we shared. As a boy he had never held firmly or deeply to the true faith and I had drawn him away from it to believe in the same superstitious, soul-destroying fallacies which brought my mother to tears over me. Now, as a man, he was my companion in error and I was utterly lost without him.

Yet in a moment... you took him from this world. For you are the God of vengeance as well as the fountain of mercy.

You follow close behind the fugitive and recall us to yourself in ways we cannot understand....

My friend fell gravely ill of a fever. His senses were numbed as he lingered in the sweat of death, and when all hope of saving him was lost, he was baptized as he lay unconscious.... New life came into him and he recovered.

And as soon as I could talk to him—which was as soon as he could talk to me, for I never left his side since we were so dependent on each other—I tried to chaff him about his baptism, thinking that he too would make fun of it, since he had received it when he was quite incapable of thought or feeling.

But his friend did not make fun of it, and after this friend did die, Augustine reflected:

I felt that our two souls had been as one, living in two bodies, and life to me was fearful because I did not want to live with only half a soul. Perhaps this, too, is why I shrank from death, for fear that one whom I had loved so well might then be wholly dead....

What madness to love a man as something more than human! What folly to grumble at the lot man has to bear! I lived in a fever, convulsed with tears and sighs that allowed me neither rest nor peace of mind. My soul was a burden, bruised and bleeding. It was tired of the man who carried it, but I found no place to set it down to rest.

Neither the charm of the countryside nor the sweet scents of a garden could soothe it. It found no peace in song or laughter, none in the company of friends at table or in the pleasures of love, none even in books or poetry. Everything that was not what my friend had been was dull and distasteful. I had heart only for sighs and tears, for in them alone I found some shred of consolation.

But if I tried to stem my tears, a heavy load of misery weighed me down. I knew, Lord, that I ought to offer it up to you, for you would heal it. But this I would not do, nor could I, especially as I did not think of you as anything real and substantial. It was not you that I believed in, but some empty figment.

The god I worshipped was my own delusion [This was before his real conversion. At this time he knew God only as a distant abstraction or as a word taught him by his mother] and if I tried to find a place to rest my burden, there was nothing there to uphold it. It only fell and weighed me down once more, so that I was still my own unhappy prisoner, unable to live in such a state yet powerless to escape from it. Where could my heart find refuge from itself?

Where could I go, yet leave myself behind? Was there any place where I should not be a prey to myself? None. But I left my native town. For my eyes were less tempted to look for my friend in a place where they had not grown used to seeing him.

So from Thagaste I went to Carthage... [Little by little time replaced the memory of his friend with fresher memories. Augustine analyzes it this way.] the grief I felt for the loss of my friend had struck so easily into my inmost heart simply because I had poured out my soul upon him, like water upon sand, loving a man who was mortal as though he were never to die.... Blessed are they who love their friends in you and their enemies for your sake. They alone will never lose those who are dear to them, for they love them in one who is never lost, in God.[10]

To lovers of the writings of the saints, equally well-known are the words of St. Bernard about the death of loved ones. His response to the death of his beloved brother, echoes that of St. Stephen at the death of the monk Alberic in 1109, so full of supernatural consolation: "Alberic is dead to our eyes, but not to the eyes of God. Dead as he seems to us, he lives for us before the Lord. For this is the way of the saints, that when they go to God by death... they carry their friends with them in their heart, there to preserve them forever; so that we may say that, death having united him to God, by an eternal and unchangeable love, he has taken us with him to God."[11]

When Bernard's beloved brother Gerard died at his monastery, Bernard delivered this famous discourse to the other monks in such open vulnerability:

Why should I dissemble what I feel?... The excess of my grief takes from me all liberty of spirit, and the blow which has fallen upon me has quenched all the light of my soul.... Hitherto I have striven, I have been able to master myself, fearing lest the sentiments of nature should overpower those of faith....

I wished to concentrate my sorrows within myself; and they became only more intense and acute. Now... my sufferings must needs come forth and be seen by others... that they may have compassion on me, and may the more tenderly console me.... It would have been better for me to die than to lose you.

[Gerard]... thou hast found far greater consolations; thou dost enjoy the immortal presence of Jesus Christ and the company of angels; but what have I to fill the void which thou hast left?...[12]

Bernard goes on to declare that he should not forget the gift he so long enjoyed and to accept the anguish as a penance. He should remember the joy of his brother in death manifesting by that joy the heaven he was entering. So he, Bernard, should rejoice in Gerard's joy and pray that his grief would be modified.

Later on in Bernard's life when a friend died, Bernard said,

"I do not lose you. I only send you before me to our Lord."[13]

St. Bernard was one of the most deeply loving saints of all times, especially in his expression of that love. As a result he suffered greatly not only from separation by death but also from any kind of distance between himself and his friends.

Off on a mission for the pope to Italy, he wrote to the monks of his home monastery:

I am obliged to labor at business which tears from me my sweet retirement. Pity my grief, and do not blame an absence to which the necessities of the Church oblige me, but in which my will has no share... let us not discourage each other; God is with us and I am with you in him.

However far distant I seem, those amongst you who are punctual to their duties, humble, fearing God, diligent in prayer, charitable toward their brethren, may rest assured that I am always with them. How should it be otherwise, being that I am, one heart and one soul with you? Whilst if there be... one monk who is unruly, discontented, reckless... even if I were present with him in body, he would be as far from my heart as he would be from that of God, through the disorder of his life.[14]

In other words we are closest to those absent in the manner of spiritual presence when we and they are being and doing good, for then we are closest to God in whom all of us find our true being.

Of sufferings of loss due to rejection, we must not forget the famous scene of the father of St. Francis dragging him before the bishop in protest of his son's flamboyant generosity to the poor. After Francis' famous disrobing to give everything back to his father, he leaves on his grace-filled adventures.

The fact that our Umbrian saint of peace was not able to find full reconciliation with his father throughout the many years to follow signifies the depth of the wound. Perhaps readers who cannot find a path to reunion with parents need to pray to St. Francis for special graces of forgiveness on both sides.

St. John of the Cross, who was known for his detachment, did love his own region of Spain and the people who lived there. When sent under obedience to Andalusia, he went humbly but then begged to be sent back to Castile saying: "Desolation cuts sharp, but behind the darkness of suffering a great light is growing."[15]

He wrote this poem during his time of "exile" in Andalusia:

All lonely her abode
Hid in a lonely nest her lovely bed.
Then on a lonely road,
By her Beloved led,
Whose heart, love-wounded, too, had lonely bled.[16]

This poem shows that St. John of the Cross found a remedy for the loneliness of homesickness in identification with the wounded heart of Christ.

In a more feminine mode, from the words of the anonymous contemplative Carmelite nun quoted in the chapter on interior trials: "When the pain of the heart is embraced and experienced, when we choose to love until the heart breaks, we discover that we are not alone, that we are never alone, that Love is a reality, that the Beloved abides in deep communion within us."

From St. Martin de Porres himself, we have no long expression of his innermost thoughts, but I think that the words Eddie Doherty gives him in his biography are put in a way that can help other readers with loneliness caused by rejection. In this case the Spanish father ignores the son of his love union with a black woman:

Ah, little son, [Mary tells the boy Martin as he prays] you are sore grieved that your father neglects you, that he will not own you as his son. And you feel shamed that you were not wellborn—as Pilate was, or Caesar who preened himself on his heredity as though he had created it by some effort of his own!

All things that live are given life by God. Life is holy, Martin. Keep it holy. No man is lowly born—though his birth occur in a stable. No soul comes carelessly from the hand of God. No human soul, though it claim centuries of noble blood, is more beloved of God than yours is, though every man on earth proclaim it illegitimate.

Pray for the man who will not own you as his son, and judge him not. God is your real father, Martin. He loves you with a love not even I, your mother, can bestow....

Mother, my breast is torn with joy!....

Feel not lonely any more, since God, your Father, is concerned for all your needs, eager to listen to you always, no matter how unworthy you may be, and solicitous to weigh your least requests.[17]

To turn back again to stories of saints bereaved, when St. Thomas More lost his first wife through an unexpected death, he was numb with pain. He accepted it in resignation, realizing that Jane belonged to God not to him, thinking in this way to imitate Christ who accepted the will of the Father in his own manner of death.[18]

St. Jane de Chantal, the disciple of St. Francis de Sales, first lost her mother when she was a child, then her dearly loved husband just before the birth of their last child. Of the four children that survived birth, three would die before Jane, one as a child and two as young adults.[19]

Wendy Wright, who introduces one edition of the *Letters of Spiritual Direction* of these two saints, believes that whereas men are threatened by intimacy, women are most threatened by separation.[20] If this be true, St. Jane is a model for survivors of so many traumas of separation in death.

De Sales, commenting about a time when Jane of Chantal offered her own life in exchange for the ebbing life of a young girl in her charge:

> I do not think it is good that you offer your life.... No, my dear daughter, we must not only accept what God strikes us with, but we must also acquiesce that it be in the manner which pleases him. We must leave the choice to God, for it belongs to him.
>
> From these temporal losses, my daughter, with which God touches the lute-strings of our heart as he chooses, will result a beautiful harmony. "Lord Jesus, without reserve, without any if, without a but, without any limitations, may your will be done, to father, mother, daughter, in all and everywhere." I do not say that we should not wish and pray for their preservation, but, my dear daughter, we should not say to God: "Leave this one and take that."[21]

By the time Francis himself would die, he who was spiritual father, friend, and everything to her, St. Jane would be ready to follow the sweet but heroic directions he had given her about other deaths. She would write to another sister:

> You say you want to know what my heart felt on that occasion [the death of St. Francis de Sales]. Ah, it seems to me that it adored God in the profound silence of its terrible anguish. Truly, I have never felt such an intense grief nor has my spirit ever received so heavy a blow.
>
> My sorrow is greater than I could ever express and it seems as though everything serves to increase my weariness.... The only thing that is left to console me is to know

that it is my God that has done this, or at least, has permitted this blow to fall. Alas. My heart is too weak to support this heavy burden, how it needs strength.

Yes, my God, you put this beautiful soul into the world, now you have taken it back; may your holy name be blessed. I don't know any other song except, "May the name of the Lord be blessed."

My soul is filled with grief but also full of the peace of God's will which I would never oppose with even the slightest resistance.... I affirm what it has pleased Him to do—to take from us that great flame that lit up this miserable world and let it shine in his kingdom, as we truly believe.... I am certainly too insignificant to merit... the contentment I had in seeing my soul held in the hands of such a great man who was truly a man of God.

I believe that God in his supreme goodness does not want me to take any more pleasure in this world and I don't want to take any more either except to hope to have the joy of seeing my dearest Father in the bosom of His everlasting goodness.[22]

Many are the women saints who lost their children. In former times it was most common for babies and older children to die of the many diseases incurable before the coming of antibiotics and other present-day remedies.

Of the death of one of her beloved daughters, St. Elizabeth Seton wrote: "It would be too selfish in us to have wished her inexpressible sufferings prolonged and her secure bliss deferred for our longer possession... though in her I have lost the little friend of my heart."[23]

Cornelia Connelly is an about-to-be-beatified holy woman whose story will be told in detail in the next chapter. Here is the dreadful account of the death of one of her children, which marked the end of a happy time in her life. Her little son was just two-and-a-half years old when the tragedy took place.

John Henry was the darling of the family, adventurous, lighthearted, and gay.... She... was standing one day in the garden watching him. Suddenly, it seemed to her that she was too fortunate, that her love for God had meant no proper sacrifice, had brought with it no special demands....

Twenty-four hours later her little son lay dying. He had run into the garden in the keen morning air with a huge Newfoundland dog. They had played together and somehow, between the large good-natured clumsiness of the dog and the young, inexpert limbs of the child, he had climbed up and fallen, or been pushed, into a boiler which was used outside the house for converting the raw maple juice into sugar. He took a long time to die. For forty-three hours, scalded and in agony, he lay in his mother's arms.

The night was protracted, interminable. But there was no bitterness, no recantation. On the following morning, as she later wrote, "at early dawn on the feast of the Purification he was taken into the temple of the Lord."

Her diary is the only witness. Three words record the night. There is little to show whether they are resigned or rebellious, given involuntarily or wrung from her by insupportable pressure—only the reiteration, like the beating of a closed fist upon the page, "Sacrifice! Sacrifice! Sacrifice!"[24]

The rest of her tragic but beautiful story carries on the same motif. We know from her holiness that somehow God's grace brought her through the death of her son with a heart made still more loving.

Conchita, Concepcion Cabrera de Armida, is a holy woman of Mexico who is about to be beatified. She also suffered bereavement: the loss of a son, a beloved husband, and a favorite daughter. When her son Carlos died at age six, she was inconsolable. Only after a long time was she able to let go of him completely into the arms of Christ, symbolized by giving away a treasured garment of his to a poor boy.

Of the death of her husband she wrote:

This sword pierced my soul, without any assuagement, without any consolation. This very night, the Lord presented to me the chalice and made me drink of it drop by drop to the dregs.

During these days, I visited the tabernacle for sustenance and strength. Oh! If I had not been sustained by him, then through my great weakness, I would have succumbed....

What a model husband! What a model father! What an upright man! What finesse, what delicacy in his relations with me, so respectful in all his actions, so Christian in all his thoughts, so honest, so perfect in everything he did!...

Oh! how ephemeral is life! How short our existence! How near to each other are the present and the past! What do we do when this time is not employed for God alone?[26]

Let us end this chapter with Praxedes, the holy Spanish woman described in our chapter about exploitation. One of the sons of Praxedes, at fourteen years old, was killed in a train accident. "Drowning in tears she cried out 'my son has died' and then 'in this world I wish to suffer as Christ suffered... my son was not mine, but God's, who was his only owner. He has chosen to take him back. All I have to do is be content with God's holy will.... May God give me more to suffer because this is not enough for me yet.' She offered many Masses and penances and one day saw a vision of him in the arms of the Blessed Virgin."[27]

Fearing that her other sons would be killed in the civil war, she devoted herself to Christ with tears and prayers and penances. She spoke of her own death as her flight to her native home.

STEPS TO FACING LONELINESS AND LOSS ENFOLDED IN CHRIST'S LOVE

1. Pray from the depths of the heart, seeking union with Christ rather than relying on formal words only. Don't be afraid to shed tears and to weep and wail, for this will open you to the consolation God will give at the time he wills.

2. Ask God for the gift of a greater sense of his presence, not for the sake of spiritual vainglory but in order to keep from falling into despair. Let him show you that he is worthy to be the bride of your soul, worthier than any beloved human. Let him help you learn to love others in his heart where there is no separation.

3. Courageously fling yourself on his providence in your neediness. For the needs of those separated from you, stir up your belief that God loves them more than you do and will bring them through their difficulties. Offer your fear as a sacrifice for the conversion of the world.

4. Ask for an increase in faith in being reunited with loved ones in eternity.

EIGHT

Meeting Christ in the Suffering of Marital Discord

Blessed are you when men revile you and persecute you and utter all kinds of evil against you falsely on my account. Rejoice and be glad, for your reward is great in heaven. Matthew 5:11-12

I am using the milder term "marital discord" to cover many sources of pain within marriages because the word discord is more all-inclusive than divorce or battering. Under the title of marital discord will be treated sufferings as extreme as murder, ranging to abandonment, divorce, infidelity, violence, raging scenes, and what we would now call psychological battering. Often such miseries have repercussions on the children as well, creating still more pain for the saint.

I use the word "her" because I have not come across any printed examples of badly treated holy husbands. But I am sure they exist.

CORNELIA CONNELLY: A SAINT FOR THE UNHAPPILY MARRIED OR DIVORCED

One of the most bizarre examples of marital discord is to be found in the life of Cornelia Connelly (1809-1879),[1] a woman whose cause for beatification is about to be concluded.

Cornelia was baptized in the Lutheran Church. Attracted by the many gifts of Pierce Connelly, an Episcopal clergyman, Cornelia entered his church and was married to him. Four years later they had thought and prayed their way into the Roman Catholic Church. Charming, intelligent, and ardent, in Rome while on pilgrimage they were welcomed with open arms by the English and American Catholics living in the eternal city.

On their return, with two little children in tow, Pierce began to teach at a Catholic college in New Orleans. The atmosphere of piety among the sisters of the school and their Jesuit advisors encouraged Cornelia to grow in the faith she had adopted originally partly to please her husband. Growing in interior love for Christ, she prayed for the graces to live a holy life as a wife and mother.

Then came the tragic death of her third child, described in our chapter on loneliness and loss. Stricken, but faithful to God, Cornelia was bearing a fourth child when to her utter amazement her beloved husband Pierce declared without warning that he wanted to become a priest![2]

How can a married father of children become a Catholic priest? In those days the only practical way would be if Cornelia wanted to become a nun. In preparation, Pierce told Cornelia they must live as brother and sister for a few years "to test his vocation and their endurance... a sober and frightening demand.... If Cornelia refused him she might be standing in the way of his proper vocation.... She was stricken and disbelieving."[3] Strangely their spiritual advisors agreed with Pierce, believing that he had a unique vocation. As a former Episcopalian, he was especially interested in reevangelizing England.

Cornelia agreed. She had to. There were too many arguments against her and, in the argument of the heart, suffering as well. There is a stage in dilemma where, if the intention is to discover and act upon the right thing, the right thing seems identifiable only with what demands most sacrifice. It was so in Cornelia's case. Her acceptance was the hardest thing ever asked of her, against which her instincts and reason rebelled.[4]

The end result of the ordination of Pierce as a Roman Catholic priest, and of her own discernments was that Cornelia's oldest son was sent to a school in England while she kept the youngest two and worked on the foundation of a new English educational order of sisters which would be called The Society of the Holy Child Jesus, known in our times as the Holy Child Sisters.

At this point a reader might still think this story unusual but perhaps happy from a religious standpoint. In 1847, the psychological battering began in earnest. His former wife firmly ensconced in the convent, but himself unhappy as a priest, Pierce decided that Cornelia should not take final vows. He did not like to think that she would belong irrevocably to Jesus instead of to him. His pretext was worry about any debts the convent might run up which he could be responsible for.[5]

Is there a separated or divorced reader of this chapter who is not grimacing at this point, fully aware of how money matters become the battling ground for estranged spouses?

When Cornelia took her religious vows in spite of Pierce's opposition, he suddenly removed their three children from the schools they were in and fled with them to Italy! Later on he would admit that his motive was to hold the children hostage to win Cornelia back. What a Catholic soap opera this story makes! It is necessary for the reader to remember at this point that the rest of the tale will be taking place in a virulently anti-Catholic England opposed to religious vows.

Naturally, Cornelia was terrified of having the children in the hands of her unbalanced husband. She had to choose between leaving the convent to remarry Pierce and be with her children or to remain in hope and prayer not knowing what was happening to them. Here is how the distraught mother met Christ in her anguish: "In union with my crucified Lord and by His most Precious Blood; in adoration, satisfaction, thanksgiving, and petition, I Cornelia vow to have no further intercourse with my children and their father, beyond what is for the greater glory of God, and is His manifest will through my director, and in case of doubt on his part through my extraordinary (confessor)."[6]

Coming back to England to fetch Cornelia and finding her unwilling even to see him, Pierce "fell weeping on the sofa (of the convent parlour) and for the next few hours remained... to rage and plead."[7] In effect, Cornelia was refusing to be blackmailed. She insisted instead that she would only talk to Pierce when he had restored at least her daughter to her.

In retaliation the frustrated former husband began to publically accuse one of Cornelia's advisors with having assaulted Cornelia and also carrying on an affair with a younger nun, claiming that the convent was a brothel.[8]

In justification for all of this, he wrote to the bishop "I am a man, a husband, and a father before I am a priest and my first duties cannot be abandoned. Faith, fidelity, and honor I will never forsake, nor will I forsake the wife I vowed to protect for life, the mother of my children."[9] This from a man who had begged Rome for permission to become a priest swearing that his wife would become a vowed religious.

To overcome the clear contradiction between his feelings and his previous decisions, Pierce would eventually come to the conclusion that the whole venture of his priesthood had been misguided. He would institute a legal case against Cornelia for abandoning him. To the Protestant English public, Cornelia would be vilified as a cold, cruel, unnatural mother.

After much wrangling the case was set aside, but only after an apparent victory for Pierce which could have resulted in a prison sentence for Cornelia unless she returned to her husband! She was advised to be ready to flee at a moment's notice. During this time of stress, Cornelia reassured her advisors that there was nothing to fear since God and truth were on her side.[10]

These miseries were further compounded by Pierce's attempts to get Cornelia's American relatives to agree that she was insane so that money left in trust for the children could be released to him. He continued to allege that Cornelia was being controlled by devilish immoral priests. Cornelia agreed to have the money sent to Pierce. Again, he begged her to return to him.

Eventually, he would return to the Episcopal ministry, living in Florence with two of the children. It is easy to imagine the terrible fears of Cornelia for the earthly and eternal future of her beloved children. Pierce was able to turn them against their mother as one stubbornly and unfeelingly choosing her unnatural vows against the love she owed to her husband and progeny!

Her elder son, Mercer, who had become a militant Protestant, would die of yellow fever at age twenty-one. Hearing the news, Cornelia broke down in tears of utter misery. Her daughter, Adeline, would write her rude letters from time to time. When grown up, Adeline and Frank, the younger son, would occasionally visit Cornelia, but only to express their anger, leaving the nun with large tears in a pool upon her lap.[11]

After Cornelia's death, through the influence of the Holy Child nuns, Adeline would reconvert to the Catholic faith.

Marital discord is no new phenomena. Of the days of the early church, we have the famous St. Fabiola, a noble Roman woman who divorced her husband because of his sexual vices. She married again even though it was against church law. When her second husband died, she became a penitent, founded many religious communities and hospitals, eventually becoming a Scripture scholar under St. Jerome.[12]

St. Monica, the mother of St. Augustine, was badly treated by her ill-tempered and lustful pagan husband. Although many husbands in those days battered their wives, Patricius refrained out of respect for Monica's gentle patient Christian ways. Eventually, he would fulfill the famous words of St. Paul "the unbelieving husband is consecrated through his wife" (1 Cor 7:14 RSV).

Another unhappily married woman saint was Radegunde of the sixth century.[13] When her father was assassinated during a political plot, the girl was carried off to the castle of King Clotaire. At eighteen she was married to Clotaire I, the first Christian King of what we know of now as France.

Although Clotaire was baptized, he was a brutish, sensual man who married five times! Unhappy in her marriage, Radegunde devoted herself to the care of the poor, the sick, and the captive. The King was not too happy about the character of his wife either. He used to say that he had married a nun rather than a queen and that she was making his court into a monastery.

Although Radegunde tried to please her difficult husband, when he had a beloved brother of hers murdered, she begged to leave the court for a convent. The Bishop hesitated about her consecration, fearing a bloody reprisal on the part of the violent King. To overcome the doubts of the Bishop, Radegunde dressed herself in the habit of a nun and demanded that he bless her.

She then journeyed to a remote estate of the King and spent all her money in charity. Later she would build a monastery in Poitiers. The King ruminated on means to drag her back but finally repented and begged her forgiveness. This conversion did not last long. He later burned alive one of his sons and his grandchildren! Again he repented and in penance donated large sums to Radegunde's monastery.

During the last years of her life, Radegunde lived in total solitude. After her death her face was resplendent with light, and healing miracles were attributed to her intercession.

Terrifying is the tale of St. Godelieve of Belgium (1049-1070). A holy child, she longed to become a cloistered nun but was married for political reasons to one Bertolf. Once in the home of her husband, Godelieve's mother-in-law, who had preferred another woman for her son, treated Godelieve brutally, confining her to a cell and all but starving her. Her husband went along with this treatment, resenting the holiness of his wife.

Godelieve escaped to her father's house and complained to the Bishop. Bertolf promised to improve in his treatment of his wife and was given permission to take her back. Instead, he went off on a trip, arranging beforehand that Godelieve be drowned by one of his servants.[14] In this way our saint died at age twenty-one of an "accidental" death.

The story has an unexpected ending. Bertolf remarried. His daughter was born blind. When her eyes were washed in the water from the pool where Godelieve had been drowned, the baby was miraculously healed. Thunderstruck by this sign of forgiveness, Bertolf confessed plotting the murder and entered a monastery where he lived a life of penance! St. Godelieve is an intercessor for family peace.

Another more cheerful story of marital discord is that of Blessed Zedislava Berka, a Bohemian of the thirteenth century.[15] Married against her will to a soldier who wanted her to dress luxuriously and attend numerous banquets, the prayerful, inward wife was most unhappy. However, she decided to try to spiritualize the worldly activities her husband demanded of her while continuing to mother her four children and devote herself to the poor.

On one occasion she brought a repulsive beggar right into the castle to tend to his needs. Hearing about it, her husband rushed furiously to the scene only to find in place of the beggar the figure of Christ crucified.

When the third order of St. Dominic began to grow in Eastern Europe, Zedislava's husband agreed that she could become a member and helped her to build a hostel for pilgrims and refugees. Gradually, he let her devote more and more time to her Christian works of mercy. After her death he would see a vision of her soul in glory which would convert him also from worldly ways of living.

One of the most famous of abused wives is St. Rita of Cascia (1381-1457). An ardent lover of Christ, Rita wanted to become a nun. She was an only child, so her parents pleaded with her to remain in the world to be their mainstay. Rita was given a divine inspiration to obey her parents' request that she marry. Rita was then given in marriage to Paolo Ferdinando, a quick-tempered, brutal man, both in town feuds and in the home. Their two sons were also of Paolo's violent temper.

Rita, by her gentle, joyful love of God, silent and forgiving, willing to bear all out of love for Christ, tried to cover over the faults of her male family members. Shortly before his death Paolo converted and tried to make up for his abusive behavior, but he became the victim of an assassin's knife. His sons pledged to avenge his death by killing his enemies. Rita begged them to practice the mercy of Jesus instead of perpetuating the feud. In despair of their plots, she finally prayed that her sons should rather die still innocent than live to commit sins of murder. Within a year, both sons died.[16]

Later Rita would become a nun, devoted to contemplation of Christ crucified. She was given the stigmata in the form of a thorn in her head.

Recently beatified is a Canadian saint, Marguerite d'Youville, whose sufferings sound familiar enough even though the setting might be more exotic.[17] This eighteenth-century foundress of the Sisters of Charity of Montreal was a child in an extremely happy, large family of French colonial origin. Against the background of her beautiful family life as a child, she would be shocked by her treatment as a wife and daughter-in-law.

A charming, pure, and beautiful young woman, Marguerite was much courted by the young men of the colony. Unlike the many stories of arranged marriages in so many lives of women saints, in this case the villain was chosen by the victim. Marguerite picked Francois d'Youville as the most fascinating and handsome man of her set.

Full of love and happiness, the bride would soon become brokenhearted as her husband became more and more cold, indifferent, and unfaithful. This came about largely because of his addiction to gambling. Instead of his delightful company, the young mother of five was abandoned into the hands of an irritable, jealous mother-in-law who despised her.

In her sufferings, Marguerite was consoled by the love of Christ who chose this time to reveal his love for her in a close mystical embrace. From that moment, her heart became detached from earthly things and she became peaceful and calm in a state of surrender. She spent less time with her friends and devoted herself to the care of her family and the poor. Though lacking worldly goods, she still was loved for her kindness, beauty, and regal dignity.

When her dissipated husband lay dying after only eight years of marriage, Marguerite grieved for him and willingly undertook to clear his name of the many debts he had contracted. She was able to bail him out through all sorts of creative business initiatives.

The generous forgiveness of Marguerite may remind you of the attitude of Praxedes Fernandez, described in the chapter about exploitation. Her remedy for physical abuse was to get advice from her father and mother-in-law, the latter shaming the husband into desisting. Content with his changed behavior, Praxedes was renewed in her love for him and greatly grieved when he died.

STEPS TO SANCTIFICATION IN THE MIDST
OF MARITAL DISCORD

Of the many trials of saints we have studied, in some ways this one is the most difficult to write about. In our times there is much disgust concerning advice to abused women that can appear to be gentle toward the husband and harshly demanding of the wife. Presumably he is to be given a light tap on the hand, and she is to be instructed simply to offer it all up without protest.

In fact, what the lives of the women saints in this chapter reveal is a choice of two different ways to be faithful to Christ in the midst of marital discord:

1. To come against victimization in the name of Christ by resisting unjust demands and attitudes. We find this exemplified in Cornelia Connelly's brave defiance of her unbalanced husband's false demands. We find it in St. Fabiola's divorce. In the life of Radegunde, we find her summoning up courage to leave her husband and to become a nun when his conduct became murderous. In the flight of Godelieve from her villainous husband, unsuccessful though it turned out, we see bravery triumph over any kind of false submissiveness. Assertiveness is demonstrated more mildly in Praxedes' decision to let others know about her husband's violence.

2. In the case of other women saints such as Zedislava, Rita, or Marguerite, suffering from opposition, brutality, or emotional abandonment was met with patient forbearance. These women so much experienced themselves as brides of Christ in their souls that they could transcend the pain caused by the attitudes of their husbands.

Sometimes women who think the Holy Spirit is calling them to protest against abuse or bring charges against their husband feel impelled to berate other unhappily married women who chose the second path of taking refuge in the love of Christ and offering their pain for their husbands, children, and other worthy intentions. Sometimes women who have chosen the second path will be frightened by the vehemence of assertive women.

Such disputes among women are understandable in a time of so much family unrest. But they do not seem fruitful. All women who are unhappy in marriage must take refuge in the Sacred Heart of Jesus and discern what is best in their particular situation.

Concerning taking action against unjust husbands, it is important not to spend years in sad complaint but instead to seek direction and counseling. Of course, in many cases, there is need for change also in the attitudes and behavior of the wife.

Often the issue of whether to choose a path of outward resistance or inward self-offering will depend on the character of the husband, the circumstances, the needs of the children, and one's own emotional survival.

NINE

Meeting Christ in the Suffering of Persecution

The souls of the just are in the hand of God, and no torment shall touch them.... they shall be greatly blessed, because God tried then and found them worthy of himself... they shall shine... the faithful shall abide with him in love; because grace and mercy are with his holy ones, and his care is with the elect. **Wisdom 3:1-9**

"Father, forgive them for they know not what they do."
Luke 23:34

Who shall separate us from the love of Christ? Shall tribulation, or distress, or persecution, or famine, or nakedness, or peril, or sword?... For I am sure that neither death, nor life... nor anything else in all creation, will be able to separate us from the love of God in Christ Jesus our Lord.
Romans 8:35-39

Sometimes when describing the fierce persecution of Christians of the early church or those of religious prisoners in communist countries, it can seem as if most of us do not suffer from persecution at all.

This is not true. We still experience many types of persecution ranging from ridicule, scorn, contempt, discrimination, and hatred based on religion, sex, race, or age. We can even consider sexual abuse a form of persecution, attacking the God-given dignity of another person for the sake of one's own gratification through harassment, incest, and rape. Persecution by demons will be described in the chapter on meeting Christ in the suffering of temptation.

The milieu of persecution varies from outright violence leading to martyrdom in the public arena, to discrimination in the workplace, ostracism within a family, and enmity within the church itself.

For many Christians of our time, several types of persecution converge in pro-life protest ministry where we face physical pain, jail sentences, and always the scorn of the pro-abortion hecklers.

The Psalms are full of prayers to God for protection against persecuting enemies. In the Old Testament, even though the promise of life after death is less prominent than in the New, we see men and women willing to die rather than to give in to enemy demands (see 2 Maccabees 7:1-2, 9-14).

In the Office of Readings (24th Week in Ordinary Time), we find this excerpt from the writings of St. Augustine (Sermon 46, 10-11):

Christians must imitate Christ's sufferings, not set their hearts on pleasures…. Yes, expect the temptations of this world, but the Lord will deliver you from them all if your heart has not abandoned him. For it was to strengthen your heart that he came to suffer and die, came to be spit upon and be crowned with thorns, came to be accused of shameful things, yet, came to be fastened to the wood of the cross. All these things he did for you, and you did nothing. He did them not for himself, but for you.

But what sort of shepherds are they who for fear of giving offense not only fail to prepare the sheep for the temptations that threaten, but even promise them worldly happiness?

God himself made no such promise to this world. On the contrary, God foretold hardship upon hardship in this world until the end of time. And you want the Christian to be exempt from these troubles?

Precisely because he is a Christian, he is destined to suffer more in this world. For the Apostle says: "All who desire to live a holy life in Christ will suffer persecution...."

Let him be in Christ, if you wish him to be a Christian. Let him turn his thoughts to sufferings, however unworthy they may be in comparison to Christ's... "He chastises every son whom he acknowledges. Let him prepare to be chastised, or else not seek to be acknowledged as a son."

It is the manner of responding to the persecution that many of the saints showed forth their faith in Christ most dramatically. I have shown St. John of the Cross as an archetype because so many readers, like him, find their enemies primarily within the church. His story, as usual, will be followed by stories and insights from the lives of other saints.

ST. JOHN OF THE CROSS: PERSECUTED BY HIS BROTHERS IN THE LORD

As most readers know, St. John of the Cross was a young priest of Spain of the sixteenth century who was seeking an order where he could spend most of his time in deep contemplation. Meeting St. Teresa of Avila whom the Lord had told to found just such reformed Carmelite houses, St. John helped her found one for men.

As the reform movement became more and more popular, it aroused the indignation of the unreformed Carmelites who wanted to remain in their more lax ways. They decided to frighten John.

One evening, after hearing confessions, John passed out beneath the massive stone archway of the Church... He was eighty yards or so from his little cottage, when suddenly a man's figure sprang up, and with all the rage of passion seeking its prey, beat the friar so severely with a stick that he was knocked down, and then the ruffian fled. When he related this incident afterwards, John added that never in his whole life had he enjoyed sweeter consolation; this time men had treated him as they had treated Jesus.[1]

In those days in Spain, church and state were joined together in a manner that empowered high Catholic leaders to make use of the secular arm to bring about their goals. When the unreformed Carmelites realized that John of the Cross was the spearhead of the reform, and that they could not persuade him to join them even by such scare tactics as described above, they decided to kidnap him with the help of the local police.

Their plan was to lock John up in one of their own monasteries.[2] John had a supernatural sense that such imprisonment was coming, but he remained peaceful about the prospect, desiring to suffer for Jesus.

Soon secular soldiers came to seize him in his cottage near Teresa's convent where he was a confessor. First they scourged him and then prepared to drag him off. Given a chance to escape, he did not make use of it, placing his confidence in God and hoping for special graces in suffering persecution for the sake of Christ.

John of the Cross was to remain a prisoner for six months in the convent of Toledo. There he was questioned by Tostados, the highest authority of the order. The matters in dispute are rather complicated but the essence was that the unreformed wanted John to agree to obey the chapter rather than the apostolic visitors. John resisted because the apostolic visitors had the higher authority and they were eager to have him promote reform convents.

John of the Cross clung to his conviction that the Holy Spirit wanted him to help bring about the reform in spite of quite terrible treatment by his enemies. Under the rules of the old Carmelites it was permissible to punish a rebel severely in order to bring him around.

Considered as a rebel, John was kept in a narrow room, six feet by ten feet with one small window. He ate dinner often on the floor of the refectory—bread and water—whipped by the friars who thought they were doing the right thing to break his disobedient spirit.

While eating, he was subject to the ridicule of his Carmelite brothers. "At every mouthful he made an act of love that he might not yield to the temptation of calumny."[3]

During this time he went through unbearable interior purification such as he described later in *The Dark Night of the Soul,* but this was followed by ecstasies so beautiful as to render his sufferings as nothing by comparison. After his escape John said "one single grace of all those which God granted me there could not be repaid by many years of imprisonment."[4]

In prison he reached the stage of spiritual marriage. Sometimes the prison area glowed with supernatural light.

At one point in John's imprisonment, Jesus came in glory to console John, saying: "I am here with thee to deliver thee from all evil." The prisoner never complained about the insults or the conditions though these were most unpleasant, for it was freezing in winter and boiling hot and stench-filled in summe

Deprived of being able to say Mass for the feast of the Assumption, Our Lady appeared to him and told him he would soon be able to leave the prison.[5] In a vision Mary showed him a window and told him she would help him escape. She instructed him on how to unscrew the locks on his prison. Once allowed to leave his cell for a short time, John looked for and found the window of the vision; looking out, he saw a drop of 150 feet to the Tagus river.

He made a rope of old coverlets and used it to descend from the window. Later it was realized that this escape had to be miraculous since the rope could not have held to the upper floor. After the drop, the voice of Mary led him to safety. He was lifted over the monastery wall onto a little street where he escaped to a convent of reformed nuns and hid in their enclosure.[6]

Safe in their community, John told the nuns that never had he enjoyed such contentment and light and sweetness as while in prison. He spoke of his enemy Carmelites as great benefactors.[7] He advised his brethren to look forward to violent persecution and even to be ready to ask others to strike harder so that they might all become martyrs for Christ.

About community life in general, John of the Cross used to say: "Look upon it as certain and advantageous that there will always be difficulties in convents and communities, for the devil never ceases from trying to bring about the fall of saints, and God allows them to be exercised and put to the proof."[8] He thought it best that community members have low expectations, acting as if they were alone in order to maintain their own peace.

After the reform was well established, John became subject to more minor forms of persecution from brethren who you would think would revere their founder. By the end of his life, he was deprived of all leadership and plans were made to confiscate his writings. Only because of the prudence of a woman disciple were these magnificent tomes saved. John taught there were three degrees of attainment in despising honor: to try to learn to despise ourselves and to wish that others should do so; to speak always to our own disadvantage and desire that others should do the same; to try to have a low opinion of ourselves and wish that others may have the same.[9]

The heroic witness of martyrs is also a great witness. Of course, there are so many of these that I can only describe a few.

Of famous women martyrs of the early church, we have St.

Agatha, St. Ceclia, Sts. Perpetua and Felicity, St. Agnes, St. Barbara, St. Lucy, and St. Anastasia.

Always they were able to overcome fear because they knew Christ as a Bridegroom and saw death, no matter how horrible the circumstances, as the entrance into the bridal chamber of delights.

Later more renowned martyrs were St. Margaret Clitherow and Blessed Margaret Ward of the English persecutions. Their stories and those of many other women martyrs can be found in my *Treasury of Women Saints.*

Of the many Asian martyrs, I want to tell about Lugartha Lee Yu Hye who died in 1801 in the Korean massacres. She was a daughter in a noble family who had vowed to live in perpetual virginity as a spouse of Christ.

In her culture a woman could not be single, and so she was married to a rich young man, also a Catholic. Imagine her delight to learn that he also had made a private vow. A priest arranged that they could be married but follow the example of Mary and Joseph and live as brother and sister.

Sentenced to exile during the persecution, Lugartha challenged the judge by words so eloquent that he decided such a valuable witness to Christianity could not remain alive but must be executed to prevent the spreading of this alien faith by means of her evangelism.

In prison she was tortured, the bones of her feet broken. On the way to her death, she encouraged her weaker companions and was the first to offer her outstretched neck to the sword.

Now comes the excerpt from the famous letter she wrote home just before her martyrdom: "Here I am on the brink of death, and I cannot express myself, yet I dearly wish to say a few words to you about what has happened, and to make my farewell to this world forever.... No further desire to live remains with me, and I think only of giving my life to God when the time comes. I have firmly resolved to do this, and the more I think of it the more I try to become worthy of it."[10]

Of course, the most famous of all women martyrs is St. Joan of Arc (1412-1431).[11] Our famous Saint Joan has the honor of being adored by brilliant anti-Catholics as well as the faithful. Mark Twain, whose biography of Joan has recently been republished by Ignatius Press, actually believed that Joan of Arc was the only good person who ever lived!

We all know the story of this peasant girl with her visions who persuaded weak royalty and cowardly or exhausted soldiers to join the battle against the English who were trying to conquer all of France for themselves. Joan's standard bore the words "Jesus, Maria."

Finally captured and brought to trial as a heretic as a means of breaking the back of the French resistance, Joan was asked by her persecutors if she was certain she was in God's grace. Joan replied with humble candor: "If I am not in a state of Grace, I pray God place me in it; if be in it, I pray God keep me so."[12]

Later, when asked whether a voice that comforted her in prison was from an angel or straight from God, Joan said "the voice was of St. Catherine and of St. Margaruerite. And their heads were crowned in a rich and precious fashion with beautiful crowns.... I saw them with my bodily eyes as well as I see you; and when they left me, I wept; and I fain would have had them take me with them too."[13]

The first time Joan was brought to the stake to be burned she recanted out of terror of fire. She said she would prefer much more to be decapitated. Afterwards, she abjured her recantation and she was again brought to be burned to death. On the way she uttered devout lamentations calling upon the Blessed Trinity, and the blessed and glorious Virgin Mary, and all the blessed saints in heaven. She asked to be given a cross to kiss, and she united her sufferings to his, putting the cross on her breast between her body and her clothing. Her last word was "Jesus."

Of male martyrs there are all the apostles, many lay Christians, some of the popes, bishops, and theologians. I will concentrate here on three who are of special interest to contemporary Catholics because of the history of the countries they suffered and died in.

We described the life of St. Thomas More in our chapter on the sufferings of confronting error. The story of his martyrdom was postponed to this section. If you recall, More was persecuted mildly long before his final stance, being discriminated against in court cases for having criticized King Henry VIII. But then Thomas More decided not to subscribe to the infamous oath of allegiance to King Henry VIII since it would be a denial of his primary loyalty to the church of Rome.

As soon as More's decision to challenge the King was made, he wrote: "I know now... that my body will never rest in such a peaceful place (as a family plot). I know that my body will be tumbled from the executioner's platform into an unmarked grave on Tower Hill; I know that my head will stand sentry atop a pike on London Bridge to appease the King's anger."[14]

When in prison, More was grateful for the poverty and solitude to turn over his whole life in his mind and give thanks to God for it. He actively wished to imitate Christ in death as well as in life.[15]

Realizing his family was overwhelmed with grief that he would not compromise to avoid death, he had his daughter watch from the jail as three Carthusian monks were on their way to martyrdom. "Lo! doest thou not see, Meg, that these blessed fathers be now as cheerfully going to their deaths as bridegrooms to their marriage?"[16]

He, himself, would go to his death with a joyful prayer on his lips, saying:

"I hope all will pray for me as I will pray for all, that we may be merrily together in heaven."[17]

So happy was he to leave this world for heaven that he was

able to kiss the executioner, intone the prayers for the dying, and jest that since his beard was surely free of guilt it should be spared the guillotine!

Our next martyr saint is Blessed Theophane Venard, a nineteenth-century French missionary to Indochina. Here is an excerpt from a letter he wrote to his sister just before his travels to the Far East:

> My darling sister,
>
> How I cried when I read your letter! Yes, I knew well the sorrow I was going to bring upon my family, and especially upon you, my dear little sister. But don't you think it cost me tears of blood, too, to take such a step and give you all such pain? Whoever cared more for home and a home life than I? All my happiness here below was centered there. But God, who had united us all in links of the tenderest affection, wished to wean me from it.[18]

After a stay in Hong Kong for his language studies, Theophane began his missionary work in 1854 in Tongking, what is now called Vietnam. For more than five years he struggled on, carrying the cross of severe illness as well as the fears connected with violent persecution of the then ten thousand fervent Asian Catholics.

All Christians were subject to a torture called the lang-tri, where first their ankles, then their knees, and then their fingers and elbows would be cut off, leaving nothing but the trunk left at the end.

In order to the bring the sacraments to the beleaguered people, Theophane would move from hiding place to hiding place with his companions: "Three missionaries, of whom one is a bishop, lying side by side, day and night, in a space of about a yard and a half square, our only light and means of breathing being three holes, the size of a little finger made in the mud wall, which our poor old woman is bound to conceal by means of faggots thrown down outside."[19]

Here are some details of the events leading to Theophane's glorious martyrdom: "In 1860 a raiding party of anti-Christians raided Theophane's hiding place, put him in a cage in preparation for a trial. During this time Theophane was able to sneak out notes to the people. He told them he was not afraid for God was with him and Mother Mary would watch over him always. He was leaning not on his own strength but on the strength of Christ who has overcome death."[20]

At this point he was still able to use his time to evangelize the guards. He wrote back to France that he held no enmity against the man who betrayed him. He saw his chains as being links to Jesus and Mary.

The custom was that anyone who agreed to step on the figure of Christ on the cross placed on the ground in front of him would be freed. When he refused, he was taken through the capital in procession in his wooden cage with a big crowd of jeering onlookers. These remarked that Theophane seemed so happy that he might have been on his way to a holiday. His joyful demeanor impressed many non-Christians.

During his trial Theophane told the judge that it would be a joy to shed his blood for the people of Vietnam. They asked him to give them the names of all the Christians who had hid him. This he refused to do. Asked again to step on Jesus on the cross, Blessed Theophane said "I am not interested in what this life has to offer. I see nothing here worth buying at the price of denying my God."[21]

Asked why he hid himself so often if he wanted to die, Venard repeated the Catholic teaching which is that we may wish to die to be with Christ but we must take normal measures to preserve life. When told that he would be decapitated, he still remained happy as a lark, as the Bishop reported. He told a guard, "My heart is too big for this world and nothing here can satisfy it."

He would astound the prison administrators with his singing: "O Mother dear, place me soon in our true home near thee." He prayed that Mary "would receive his head as it fell under the axe as a bunch of ripe grapes in the vintage, as a full-blown rose which has been picked in your honor."[22]

Indeed, Theophane sang joyful hymns all the way to the execution.

Another very happy saint who would die for his faith was Padre Pro of Mexico (1891-1927).[23] Miguel Pro had been a sickly baby but a strong youth, much beloved for his clownish ways. He was always amusing the people of the neighborhood with impersonations and skits.

He became a Jesuit priest and exercised his ministry during the troubled times of the Mexican anticlerical persecutions of the church. Conditions made his past acting hobbies useful, for he could easily disguise himself as a flashy, rakish worker with a cigarette dangling impudently from the corner of his mouth as he whistled his way down the streets on his bicycle with the secret purpose of saying underground Masses and hearing confessions.[24]

When he knew that he would soon be caught and shot, he wrote a prayer to Our Lady: "I do not wish in the road of my life to savor the happinesses of Bethlehem, adoring the Child Jesus in your virginal arms. I do not wish to enjoy the amiable presence of Jesus Christ in the humble little house of Nazareth... I covet the jeers and mockery of Calvary; the slow agony of your Son, the depreciation, the ignominy, the infamy of His Cross. I wish to stand at your side, Most Sorrowful Virgin, strengthening my spirit with your tears, consuming my sacrifice with your martyrdom, sustaining my heart with your solitude, loving my God and your God with the immolation of my being."[25]

He would die from the bullets of a firing squad shouting out "Viva Cristo Rey!"

Equally moving is the story of St. Maximilian Kolbe, who died in a concentration camp in Auschwitz, Poland, during World War II.[26]

Born in 1894 to a poor family in Southern Poland, the boy who would become St. Maximilian Kolbe had a vision in which the Blessed Virgin asked him if he would take one of two crowns—white for purity or red for martyrdom. He chose both.

A most intelligent student, he had a special interest in mathematics and also in ideas for future inventions, dreaming about how to reach the moon. He entered the minor seminary of the Franciscans and would eventually make use of his technical interests in a special apostolate as the printer and publisher of widely circulating devotional magazines and books centering around the spirituality of the Immaculata.

As we will see in our chapter about physical pain, Maximilian manifested his holiness way before his death in the camps by his indefatigable zeal, working long hours in terrible conditions while encumbered by physical pain that would have kept any other man out of circulation entirely.

Here I want to relate the beautiful story of his death. Sent to the concentration camps during World War II as the sort of heroic independent figure the Nazis could never tolerate, Kolbe continued his nonstop ministry to humanity, giving the sacraments to as many as possible, and bearing the atrocious burdens of the life with serene resignation and helpfulness to others.

It was the custom at Auschwitz that if a prisoner escaped, the rest would be punished by a random selection of victims to be thrown into a bunker to starve to death. When one of these prisoners about to be hauled off cried out "my wife and my children," Kolbe moved forward and volunteered to replace him, stating that he being without a family and old and weak should be taken instead.

The victims were thrown naked into the starvation cell where there was no furniture but only a concrete floor. Kolbe made of this hellhole—which his biographer, Patricia Treece calls "the tabernacle,"—a foretaste of heaven! In the beginning of their ordeal, the other prisoners were "screaming in despair and cursing. Kolbe pacified them, heard their confessions, and prayed aloud, his voice carrying to other starvation bunkers [where those who heard him joined] in the rosary, psalms, and hymns." This was reported by a prison interpreter.[27]

The guards whose job it was to take away the corpses as the prisoners died of hunger told of the group in Father Kolbe's cell being so absorbed in prayer they did not hear the door being opened. So penetrating was the glance of the saint that they had to insist that he look at the ground and not at them. While the others slowly succumbed in their weakness, Father Kolbe remained standing or kneeling, his face serene. When given a final deadly injection to speed up the dying process, the face of Kolbe was radiant.

Maximilian Kolbe was canonized in 1982.

It might seem an anti-climax to describe at this point the sufferings of still more saints as they tried to meet Jesus in the midst of persecution, but I think they are so interesting that you will want to read about them even in brief.

St. Benedict was persecuted by monks who thought him too strict. They tried to poison him. He blessed the cup with the sign of the cross and it shattered.[28]

It is said that Saint Bernard was never impatient or out of humor no matter how ill he was treated. He prayed for those who accused him in so efficacious a manner that it was jokingly said it was a blessing to be his enemy![29]

Once Bernard was travelling through a forest. He was assailed by a troop of robbers who took away his horse and stripped him. One of the robbers returned to the site to see how the victim had reacted. When he saw him praying that God pardon them, this robber was conscience stricken. The whole group agreed to return and give back what they had taken and ask pardon of St. Bernard.

Yet when accused by a cardinal of being a troublesome frog issuing from a marsh to trouble the Holy See, St. Bernard defended himself with holy boldness for obeying higher authorities contrary to his own inclination to solitude. This led to a change of heart of his enemies who repented and defended him afterwards.

When persecuted by his own monks after they were given high offices in the church, he considered that this was a punishment for being too attached to the consolation of their friendship... that he was to learn to hope for nothing from people.[30]

Some of us might do well to hang the following passage from the writings of St. Bernard where it can often be seen: "I am little concerned at being condemned by those who call good evil, and evil good; who take light for darkness, and darkness for light... it is an honor for me to be, in some degree, united to Jesus Christ who was insulted and reviled."[31]

St. Francis of Assisi is a fine archetype for how to meet Christ in the suffering of ridicule by family members. I am sure you recall the famous story, but it is always delightful to retell it again.

When Jesus told our medieval Italian, Francis of Assisi, to rebuild his church, the youth took it literally, selling his horse and some of his father's bales of cloth to buy supplies. His father was furious and locked Francis in the cellar. When Francis was released to face the bishop's court, he was told to restore the money to his father.

Francis replied: "Up to this time I have called Pietro Bernardone father, but now I am the servant of God. Not only the money but everything that can be called his I will restore to my father, even the very clothes he has given me." He threw off all his garments save his hairshirt.

Three years before his death, Francis of Assisi said to Brother Elias: "You must consider it a grace when the brethren, as well as other men, are against you. You should actually desire it. And you should love those who are opposed to you and desire nothing but what the Lord wills."[32]

St. Catherine of Siena used to cope with contemptuous people by suddenly reading their minds to their amazement. This would usually lead them to repent of their ill thoughts of the saint. So often did this happen that Catherine used to have a confessor on hand to relieve curiosity-seeking ridiculers of the sins she saw hidden in their souls!

St. Ignatius Loyola was persecuted for speaking of spiritual matters before getting an academic degree. Imprisoned he was let go and told to avoid all novelties. "I should never have supposed," Ignatius answered simply, "that it was a novelty among Christians to speak of Jesus Christ."[33]

When an influential cardinal in Rome sought to prevent the approval of the Society of Jesus, Ignatius had several thousand Masses said, after which his opponent agreed to the foundation.[34]

During a time of difficulties when it was thought that the order might be dissolved by the pope, Ignatius naturally felt upset. He examined himself in prayer and said: "If this misfortune were to fall upon me, provided it had not happened by my fault, even if the society were to melt like salt in water, I believe that a quarter of an hour's recollection in God would be sufficient to console me and to re-establish peace within me."[35]

Concerning ridicule, Ignatius taught that it was not a good idea to seek relief by making fun in return of the one who is bothering you. He thought that enjoying taking revenge on opponents by telling others of their faults ricochets in a negative way upon the speaker, for it proves that one prefers to speak about the work of the devil than about God's work in the good deeds of others!

St. Teresa of Avila was ridiculed and scorned by a lax community of nuns. They arranged for the excommunication of the nuns who had voted her in! In this trouble Teresa leaned on the powerful friendship of Gracian.[36] She taught that the most painful trials of rejection come not from enemies but from friends, but that as we advance in prayer we come to love our persecutors.

During the Spanish Civil War, Jose Escriva had to hide in horrible places including a madhouse. It was for him a time of prayer and penance. He advised his followers that in times of persecution or when you feel your personality is eclipsed by harsh criticism and ridicule, one should keep working, confident that things will change with greater fruit than before. When slandered "say nothing, pray, work, smile."

Some of the most moving examples of forgiveness of persecutors occurs in the stories of saints who were victimized by sexual abuse in the context of incest or of rape. To give some examples of saints threatened by incest, we have St. Susanna, St. Dymphna, and St. Winifred of Wales. The victims of actual rape include St. Agnes, St. Zita, St. Joan of Arc, Blessed Pierina Morosini, and Blessed Antonia Mesina. For more about these incidents see my *Treasury of Women Saints.*

The most famous of saints threatened by rape was St. Maria Goretti, whose life seems so prophetic of a century of so much sexual violence not only in the midst of wars but also within families and neighborhoods.

Born in 1890, Maria was the eldest girl in a poor farming family. Barely able to make a living off the farm, the Gorettis took in borders: one Serenelli and his fourteen-year-old son, Alessandro. This boy had become worldly when sent as a lad to work at the waterfront of Ancona. The two families lived in an old bar separated into small rooms.

The devout Maria, who spent her days helping her mother with the children and the chores, had been taught that it was better to die than to commit a mortal sin. When her father died, she was only nine years old. By the time she was twelve,

Alessandro became attracted to the comeliness of the young girl living in such close proximity. He used to adorn his room with pornographic pictures, and as his lust increased, he was driven wild with desire.

Finally he threatened Maria that he would kill her if she told Vyone of his attempts to seduce her. On July 5, 1902, the girl happened to be alone in the house caring for the baby. Alessandro came back from the field suddenly, sharpened a knife, and insisted Maria come inside with him. When she refused, he dragged her into the kitchen. She begged him to stop, warning him of the punishments of hell. Sobbing she tried to cover her body. He gagged her to stop her screaming, and when he saw that she would not let him rape her, he stabbed her fourteen times.

After twenty hours of excruciating pain, Maria made her final confession and forgave him publically with all her heart saying that she wanted him to be with her in heaven.

For thirty years in prison, Alessandro was to rue his murderous deed. After receiving visions of Maria from heaven forgiving him, Alessandro repented and sequestered himself in a Capuchin monastery to spend the rest of his life as a penitent.[35]

STEPS TO MEETING CHRIST IN THE SUFFERING OF PERSECUTION

1. Sometimes persecution is to be avoided for a time even if later there is no escape. Mary and Joseph fled from Herod. Jesus disappeared in the crowd who were trying to throw him off a cliff. Many of the early members of the church fled to distant lands to avoid persecution including St. Paul who was lowered down the city wall in a basket. In such cases we meet Christ as we beg him for a way to freedom, and then thank him for saving us from enemy attack.

2. The most common feature in the lives of persecuted saints is the vividness of their faith that they are confident they would meet Christ in heaven if their enemies put them to death. Years of joyful meditation on their Redeemer would make them long for death rather than cowering in attempts to avoid it.

3. In imitation of Christ who prayed from the cross, "Father, forgive them, they know not what they do," all the saints always prayed for their enemies, truly feeling sorry that these opponents did not know the Lord as intimately as they did.

4. In the case of more minor persecutions such as ridicule and scorn, which in the long run can be just as bitter as death, the saints respond in different ways. Sometimes they come against taunters with humor or assertiveness, but usually they offer the difficulties in intercessory prayer for their adversaries and for the coming of the Kingdom.

TEN

Meeting Christ in the Suffering of Confrontation with Error

Hot indignation seizes me because of the wicked.
Psalm 119:53

My eyes shed streams of tears because men do not keep thy law. **Psalm 119:136**

Zeal for thy house has consumed me. **Psalm 69:9**

A s I begin this chapter, I bring to mind certain persons of my acquaintance who would never think to include a chapter on confronting error in a book about suffering. Such Christians consider those in error simply as unfortunate people to be pitied. Hearing false ideas about the family and the church in the media is cause for consternation, but never for fierce rage and even hatred of those who oppose our Lord and his truth.

To those of us who regard false teaching as poison for the soul, the suffering of having to endure it and battle it can be a source of terrible pain. It is a problem we can scarcely get away from in times where ideas are as polarized and public as ours. Practically every day we will meet with error at least once in the speech of our associates or in the media.

What can mighty holy defenders of the faith, who flourished in past times, teach us about how to defend truth without being consumed in rage against false prophets and against those in authority who tolerate such purveyors of error?

ST. THOMAS MORE'S CONFRONTATION OF ERROR IN THE SPIRIT OF CHRIST

The life of St. Thomas More of the sixteenth century is well-known to many Catholics because of the stage-play and movie *Man for All Seasons.* He is also frequently cited as a lay saint, for he was twice-married and a father. Thomas More died a martyr, one of the few high placed officials of government to protest immediately against the anti-Catholic acts of King Henry VIII. The King, as you will recall, insisted that everyone affirm the legality of a remarriage of Henry considered invalid by the pope.

Before reviewing the marvelous manner of More's confrontation with the errors surrounding the reign of King Henry VIII, it will be good to recount some of his earlier experiences in times as disruptive as ours.

Born in 1478 in London into a legal family, Thomas More, became a page in the service of the Archbishop Lord Chancellor at the age of twelve.[1] I should mention that he was always very small for his age. Some readers might have heard the theory that shorter men tend to compensate for a sense of physical inferiority by intellectual combativeness, and certainly More illustrates that contention.

Thomas' greatest wish as a youth was to become an important writer. Not having the wealth to devote to this gentleman's occupation, he was forced to study at Oxford as a scholar and later for the legal profession even though the latter was detestable to him. The fact that he disliked the ways of law increased his tendency to be irascible during informal student debates of contemporary issues.

Partly to escape from the necessity of continuing in law to please his father, Thomas took refuge in the hope of becoming a Carthusian monk. While a law student, he lived in the Carthusian guest house. He was ardently religious, wearing a hairshirt from the age of eighteen and constantly pondering Scripture to see how to fulfill the loving teachings of Jesus in his busy life.

As a married man he would attend daily Mass, insist that the whole household meet for daily prayer and extend himself constantly in care for the poor and the sick. It was the custom of the town that when any women went into labor, More should be informed so that he could intercede in prayer until the delivery of the baby was announced.

The Carthusians always doubted whether More had a vocation as a monk. They were sure that so enormously gifted a scholar, speaker, and writer was meant to play a large role in the world. They were also concerned about his melancholic scruples to which I have alluded in my chapter about interior sufferings. The immediate reason for his leaving the monastery was his delight in one Jane Colt, the daughter of a landowner who equally loved young More.

Shortly after his marriage More was made a member of the King's new parliament. The sufferings of confrontation with error followed immediately. Thomas began to object publicly to the way King Henry VII's greed stood in the way of justice for the poor. His boldness resulted in retaliation as the judges friendly to the King made sure that More lost his private law cases no matter how eloquent and just they were.

Unsure, under the circumstances, if he would be able to support his growing family in the legal profession, he decided to devote more time to writing. Readers with experience of young children will smile to find that More was frustrated in attempts to pursue a literary career amidst the din of the nursery. Some marital discord was created by his preference for his work over the need of his wife for help with the children.

Humiliated by the failure of his first book, he returned to the practice of law, rendered more favorable due to the attitudes of the generous and learned new King, Henry VIII. More would come to think that the conflict between the professions of law and of writing was a matter of giving up his proud desire to live as he wished, for the sake of submitting to God's evident will that he be active in public affairs.

When his beloved first wife died, he shocked society by immediately marrying his wife's best friend, an older woman of an extremely practical nature, mostly because she was adored by the children. During this time he decided that he could only do justice to the needs of his children by giving up perfectionism in what little writing he could do and devoting more time to the prayer that would make him more patient with the family. This was especially important because he undertook their education himself. Most Catholics would think he made a good choice because even though the writings of Thomas More, such as his *Utopia*, are interesting and his religious writings deep and well thought-out, the holiness of his character has been his most important influence.

Soon the King, who treated More like a friend, began to demand more and more services of this talented, so likable courtier. His positions included Commissioner of Sewers, Aide to an Embassy to Holland, Judge, and eventually Lord Chancellor. These leadership roles led to considerable wealth. His high position, however, never led More to stop praying, fasting, and helping the poor. Politics for him was largely a matter of mediating justice to the lower classes.

Considering the miseries to follow it is significant that one of the reasons More loved the King so much was that His Highness proclaimed that in his reign God would be served first, and the King second. In fact, until his marital difficulties interfered, Henry VIII was an unusually loyal Catholic, whose book against the teachings of Martin Luther earned him the title of Defender of the Faith.

Before the great confrontation with Henry VIII, Thomas More had another most significant experience of confronting error. This concerned a son-in-law, Roper, who became fiercely anti-clerical and began to defend Lutheranism, refusing to go to Mass or pray with the family.

More reacted at first with defensive logic, but then seeing that the debates made him inordinately angry, he resorted to prayer and fasting.[2] When the famous Cardinal Wolsey threatened the young man with arrest because Roper was preaching his heresies in the streets, More prayed for the grace to remain silent, quite a wish for a man in love with words as was Thomas. So effective was More's prayer that all of a sudden Roper returned to confession and communion in the Roman Catholic Church.

Now comes the sad tale of how King Henry VIII, desperately desirous of having a son as heir, and unable to sire one with his wife Catherine, decided to find a way to declare this marriage invalid so that he could marry Lady Anne Boleyn. The ins and outs of his claim are more complicated than can readily be summarized here.

Basically, Henry tried to show that since the Old Testament forbids marrying the widow of one's brother, the church at Rome had no right to dispense the widowed Catherine to marry Henry, her first husband's brother. If Rome's dispensation was invalid, then Henry's marriage to Catherine was void, and he would be free to marry Anne.

Not a man to court martyrdom, Thomas More tried in every way to avoid giving an opinion about Henry's plans. When directly asked, he would claim that he had no viewpoint because he was not an expert in canon law. When pressed personally by Henry himself, More was forced to admit that he thought such matters were legitimately the purview of Rome.

The whole issue became a dispute between nobles and lawyers versus church and commoners, for the nobles were always jealous of the power and wealth of the church. In defending the King against the cardinals and bishops, they would eventually find a way to assume for themselves all the riches and positions held by churchmen, including the lands of the monasteries.

It is important to understand this aspect of the English dispute because those who hate institutional religion often point to the wars between Catholics, Anglicans, and Protestants as proving how quickly religious fervor leads to bloodshed. Usually the underlying cause of the wars is the greed that remains in only halfheartedly devout members of different churches, rather than being caused by matters of faith alone.

When the King demanded that More study the matter of his previous marriage to Catherine carefully and make his view public, Thomas read first the scholars who supported the King. In this way we see that far from being eager to see error everywhere, like a heresy-hunter, More was scrupulously fair and moderate.[3]

St. Thomas More would have liked to conclude that the King was right. Throughout the calamitous proceedings he always opposed not the persons who were persecuting him but their false ideas. Because of this forbearance he could easily deal with the charges against him with humor rather than rancor.

But, in fact, the more he studied the King's claims, the more he found himself opposed. The Fathers obviously taught that the church has authority to dispense. While researching the problem, More came upon a passage from St. Augustine insisting on the wrongness of failing to reprove another through fear of jeopardizing one's own interests.[4]

Although still not coming out publicly against the King, things became more and more difficult for More when the

King began to call treasonous anyone who failed to take an oath of fealty: "I will serve thee faithfully... in so far as my conscience and the law of God permits."

The wording was ambiguous. Clergy who wanted to side with the King thought they could take the oath, claiming that the conscience clause mitigated the true nature of the oath which would put loyalty to the King above loyalty to the pope. The King won most of the common people to his side by promising material rewards for fealty. The clergy had to pay huge fines as well as recognize the King as the head of the Church of England in order to avoid the death penalty.

What was Thomas More to do? Here was a man convinced of the authority of the pope as a devout Catholic. Yet he also loved his own life and did not want to abandon his family for the Tower and almost certain martyrdom. Why shouldn't he go along with almost all the clergy in taking the oath of fealty to the King with interior reservations? Indeed, the question for potential martyrs of all ages is whether to renounce the faith by giving persecutors some proof of loyalty or get around the issue, as many Christians do, by claiming the proof of loyalty to the worldly power to be just a matter of form.

More prayed that God would be merciful to all the traitorous and weak men who took the oath of fealty to the King. He begged to retire from office as he was too ill to continue as chancellor. But the King wanted More, especially, to sign the oath as a proof that so virtuous a man was not against him.

More knew that he could not consent, yet he shuddered at the suffering to his family. Finally, strengthened by God's grace he overcame his fears and spoke in the House of Lords against a bill proclaiming the King head of the Church. More was deposed from office, yet the King still asked his old friend to pray for him. The saint pitied the King who had become so much a servant to the flesh as to turn traitor to Christ's Church for love of a woman and desire for a son.

Very shortly the family began to suffer the loss of their wealth; but wanting to follow Thomas in holiness, they submitted gaily to these impoverishments. Still, they were terrified of seeing their beloved husband and father become a martyr, and they pleaded with him to sign the oath.

When accused by the King of writing a book against him, More quietly wrote to the authorities that he had not written such a book nor engaged in defensive polemics. At the trial he spoke little of the King's wrong, and when sentenced he prayed that just as St. Paul had persecuted St. Stephen and yet both now were "twain holy saints in heaven" where they could continue their friendship forever, so he trusted that his judges might yet in heaven meet merrily with him in everlasting salvation.

So peaceful was this man who in early life was so impulsive and angry in debate that he could sincerely thank the King for commuting his sentence from hanging and quartering to beheading![5]

The story of More's glorious martyrdom in 1535 was covered in our preceding chapter on meeting Christ in the suffering of persecution.

Some other examples of saints confronting error in holy ways and their sayings about how to do it will be given now.

St. Barsanuphius of the sixth-century Greek church, living in a time of many theological controversies, advised "If a man is firm in faith he will never be confused in discussions and disputes with heretics or unbelievers because he has in him Jesus, the Lord of peace and quiet. After a peaceful discussion, such a man can lovingly bring many heretics and unbelievers to the knowledge of Jesus Christ Our Saviour."[6]

St. Benedict, the sixth-century founder of the Benedictine order with a Rule that is still being followed today,[7] thought that one way to avoid vexatious disputes of all kinds was to flee from the world to a monastery. This he decided after years of studying in the turmoil of Rome. He told his monks not to meddle in worldly affairs, but instead to meet the evils of the day by charity for the poor.[8]

Chapter LXIV of the Rule says that "in administering correction, let him [the abbot] act prudently and not go to excess; lest being too zealous in removing the rust, he break the vessel. Let him study rather to be loved than feared. The abbot should be discreet and modest, expecting to learn even from the youngest."[9]

In dealing with a Goth king who visited him out of curiosity to see Benedict's miracles, the founder proved his giftedness by proclaiming secrets of the King and then urged the king to change his wicked conduct.[10]

The life of St. Bernard, one of the most amazing defenders of the faith, provides many helpful patterns for our consideration.[11] In dealing with the many heresies of his day, this twelfth-century Cistercian abbot was always mostly concerned with the salvation of souls rather than winning a victory for himself. He always tried to instruct and heal rather than dispute and discuss.

While the context of Bernard's interventions are rather horrifying, his attitudes are most edifying. For example, in confronting zealots who wanted to use force to persuade Jewish people to convert, Bernard insisted that all non-Catholics should be won over by persuasion rather than violence.[12]

Bernard, who preferred to live far from the world in a monastery, was called upon by popes and bishops to try to reconcile anti-popes. He was also ordered to confront an epidemic of heresies attacking the truths of the church by denying ecclesial authority, questioning the goodness of marriage, and the validity of the Old Testament. One such defiant hero pretended to be Jesus Christ himself.[13]

Especially difficult to deal with was the rationalism of Abelard, a theologian attractive to many because of his spirit of independence from authority and exaltation of humanity.

Instead of relying only on the pen, Bernard went to see him personally. So persuasive was St. Bernard that Abelard promised to reform. After the visit was over, however, Abelard circulated secret writings just as bad as his former ones.

Next, Bernard, in his dispute with Abelard, addressed letters to the bishops, cardinals, and the Pope telling them to take action because the faith was in peril. In his letters he relied solidly on Scripture and the Fathers. Abelard, in turn, asked for a council of bishops to defend the faith against Bernard in person.[14]

Once together before the bishops and kings, Abelard was literally unable to talk! Abelard then appealed to the pope who condemned his writings and silenced him. In victory Bernard did not gloat but sighed over the miseries of life and the burdens of disputation. Eventually, Abelard sincerely repented and finally retired to a monastery where he was reconciled to Bernard in a reunion full of affection and esteem.

Once Bernard visited Albi, an Italian town so anti-Catholic that, prior to Bernard's arrival, only thirty persons attended the mass of a cardinal. Yet when Bernard came, they all turned out because of curiosity about this famous wonder-working monk.[15] Bernard took the trouble of explaining Catholic doctrine carefully. And then, speaking from a heart full of love he asked them to signal that they had returned to the unity of the church by raising their right hand to heaven—which they did! In another town he passed out blessed bread saying that God would make sure that all who ate the bread would be healed as a sign of the truth of the faith. And this actually happened just as he said.

St. Dominic also had many a confrontation with heretical error.[16] On a trip to Toulouse, France, he noticed that many churches were abandoned. Talking to the people, he discovered that even many of the best former Catholics had been carried away by the errors of the Carthari. St. Dominic used to groan at night with appeals to the mercy of God.

Once, arrived at Toulouse, Dominic found that his landlord was a convinced heretic. Instead of simply arguing with him, Dominic first gave him the benefit of the doubt by listening to him, taking seriously all the sins of Catholics that would make any man think some other way of faith was better. Dominic, himself a man devoted to holy reform, would, by his own example, be an ideal model of what grace could do within the mother church. Identifying with the landlord's deepest aspirations but gently redirecting him in favor of Catholic reform, Dominic was able to bring the landlord back to the fold.

Probably St. Thomas Aquinas, the great Dominican Doctor of the Church, heard the tale of St. Dominic and the landlord in his novitiate. In the realm of academic philosophy and theology, he would exemplify Dominic's forbearance by beginning the consideration of any disputed question with a careful analysis of every single viewpoint he could think of that militated against the truth. Having shown his opponents that he understood their ideas so well as to be able defend their positions even better than they could, he would then launch into a disquisition about the truth itself based on the authority of Scripture and Tradition and on human reasoning. Then he would take the trouble to refute, one by one, each view of his opponents. Readers interested in studying Thomas Aquinas' methods and in enriching their minds with the truths of the faith, should study his *Summa Theologica*.

To turn to another saint who had to confront many errors of his time, Ignatius of Loyola, founder of the Society of Jesus, advised those of his company who were going to the Council of Trent that they should not be too eager to speak but be prudent and loving, quiet and attentive in listening, so that by catching the spirit and intent of others they would know when it was good to speak or to be silent. "You ought always, to the best of your power, to act so that no one may depart less inclined to peace after your speech than he was at first."[17]

He also urged them to consider in all their work that anything said in private could become public. He advised them to take up works of charity between sessions so as to prove their love for God.

Let us leap ahead to Venerable Jose Escriva, a priest of our century, founder of Opus Dei, who was often brought into confrontation with errors of dissent coming after the Council of Vatican II. When battling with error, Escriva always had recourse to prayer and mortification. Pilgrimages to Marian shrines were also a source of strength in the midst of controversy.

When discouraged, he would abandon everything to Christ saying, "All my work is for your church," begging him to save his people. He used to say, "To speak badly of others is to create an infection that poisons and undermines the apostolate. It runs counter to charity, means a useless expenditure of strength, and brings about the destruction of interior peace and loss of union with God."[18]

STEPS IN CONFRONTING ERROR IN A CHRISTIAN SPIRIT

Let us analyze the story of St. Thomas More and the others saints described in this chapter as to how to confront error without becoming drawn into bitter, raging battles that harm one's own soul and do little to convert others. If we do so, we will find some steps we can imitate:

1. Give the person in error the benefit of the doubt, rather than immediately assuming the worst about his or her ideas and motives.

2. Sometimes we think we are praying for our enemies because we mention their names hurriedly on a long list of

petitions. Sometimes we forget to pray for them at all, probably because we have already sent them to hell forever in our own judgments. Following the lead of the saints, we should pray in depth for the persons holding opposing views.

3. We should pray to the Holy Spirit for the grace to "speak the truth in love" (Eph 4:15). This can only be done if we truly hate the error but love the one who errs versus making each recollection of the person's errors an excuse for hating him or her the more.

4. Expect vindication from God not from people. We would not mind the errors of others so much if we were convinced we would be the victorious on earth. Only when our entire trust is in God, believing that it is his truth not ours, can we become peaceful and loving in our manner of coming against errors that cause so much evil and suffering for others.

In one second, Christ can have mercy on those who have been taken in by devious ideas. He can snatch them out of the hands of the devil in spite of the visible triumph of error. Not to believe that God wins in the end is not to believe at all. Not to believe that our offering of sufferings caused by error for the sake of sinners can be efficacious, is not to believe at all! And if we do not have such faith, then why are we battling for his kingdom in the first place?

Let us show our faith, then, by always offering the suffering of confronting error for the ultimate salvation of our opponents and their followers.

ELEVEN

Meeting Christ in the Suffering of Physical Pain and Fatigue

Forsake me not when my strength is spent. Psalm 71:9

Come to me all you who labour and are heavy laden and I will give you rest. Matthew 11:28

It makes me happy to suffer for you, as I am suffering now, and in my own body to do what I can to make up all that has still to be undergone by Christ for the sake of his body, the Church. Colossians 1:24

Jesus healed many sufferers of physical illness and pain (Mt 4:23) such as the man born blind, the lepers, Peter's mother-in-law, and the woman with the flow of blood. Some Christians conclude that the only way to meet the Lord in disability and pain is by praying for healing.

Everyone who is afflicted with physical handicaps, sickness, or fatique should pray to Jesus for healing. However, since so many holy people pray for healing without any change in their bodily state of infirmity, it seems clear that Jesus does not choose to heal in every case. Sometimes our pain is allowed by him for the sake of our own sanctification or to be offered for the sins of the world.

In this chapter the concentration will be on meeting Christ in bodily pain of an acute variety, but there will also be references to saints who suffered from chronic ailments and from long periods of tiredness or the mental fatigue that comes from overwork.

LYDWINE OF SCHIEDAM: A SAINT FOR THE AFFLICTED

The story given here of St. Lydwine of Schiedam is based on a book by J.K. Huysmans.[1] Huysmans' account of the life of this saint is as accurate as it is extraordinary, based on information from a relative of St. Lydwine who lived in her house for years, as well as from the writings of Lydwine's last confessor, eyewitness accounts of those who knew her, and official documents from the Burgomasters of Scheidam.[2]

Lydwine, a saint of Holland, lived between the years 1380-1433. She was a contemporary of Joan of Arc, of the same historical era of ferocious battles between royal families. Other horrors were decimating plagues and the conflicts between the anti-popes.

Lydwine would offer her phenomenal sufferings in expiation for the sins of people she knew from her town, for the souls in purgatory, for the abominations of schism, and for the excesses of clerics, monks, kings, and common people. She was lovingly supported by brothers living under the rule of St. Augustine who were founding numerous monasteries in Holland to overcome the evils of the times.

Lydwine was born in Schiedam near the Hague. She was the fourth child and only daughter of a family that had eight sons.

Lydwine wanted to live for God alone. As in so many other stories of saints, Lydwine's parents stood against her vocation. They wanted her to marry. Since the girl was so beautiful and sweet, it seemed as she would have no trouble fulfilling the dreams of her mother and father for a good marriage.

In an effort to evade their wishes, Lydwine begged God to make her ugly.[3] At fifteen she contracted an illness which left her thin, hollow faced and greenish in color. The green turned to ash gray as she began to recover. She was so weak she could not leave her room.

You might think that our young saint was kind of neurotic or morbid, but this was not really so. Lydwine had a merry temperament and loved to be outside with her friends. She especially enjoyed ice-skating. So, even though she was not completely well yet, she followed her desire and set out for the pond to skate. Unfortunately, or providentially, depending on your point of view, the poor girl was dashed against the ice, breaking a rib in the process.

The break led to a tumor and then to agonizing pain. Strangely, none of the usual medical remedies helped. After quite a time of trying different doctors, the most famous expert visited Lydwine. To everyone's astonishment, he examined her and proclaimed that her illnesses were from God for the sake of expiating the sins of the world. Because of their supernatural origin, no medical procedures could help her!

Now follows the descriptions of the pain of this Dutch saint, truly unbelievable in their severity.

She could neither lie, nor sit, nor stand, so great was the pain in any of these positions. Lydwine vomited often,

> dragging herself on her knees, rolling on her stomach... burning with fever... for three years... to perfect her martyrdom she was abandoned by those who until then had come from time to time to visit her. The sight of her agony, her groans and cries, the horrible mask of her face, drove her visitors away... her family helped her, her father's kindness never failed... but her mother... was often harsh with her

(since she was such an extra burden in an already overtaxed family.)

... the wound under her rib, which was never healed, swelled up, and gangrene declared itself... worms moved under the skin of the stomach and spread over three ulcers... they were large and black... two hundred worms were drawn out after one remedy.

Later came violent neuralgic pains in the temples... her right eye was extinguished, the other bled, violent toothache and blood flowing from mouth, ears and nose... gall stones, cancers all over, putrefaction of the marrow and dropsy after the ulcers were healed.[4]

These calamities Lydwine endured for thirty-eight years without an instant's respite. All these ills were characteristic of the plagues then rampant. Yet all her wounds, which made her hideous, exuded an odor of perfume, something like cinnamon and spices![5]

Did Lydwine accept all this right away with saintly resignation?[6] She wept and fought and almost fell into despair from envy of healthy people. She would cry when she heard the laughter of her friends at play in the streets. During the first four years she thought she was damned. She had no consolations or insights into God's plan for her. She thought God refused to hear her prayers and that her pain was worthless.

Help came in the form of the counsel of a priest. He told Lydwine that she was to suffer for souls as Jesus suffered. She should not think that she was suffering for her own sins but for those of others, in imitation of Jesus who suffered though being without sin. "And if these souls, [such as Lydwine] capable like their Creator (Saviour, Jesus) of being chastised for the crimes of which they are not guilty would not exist, it would be with the universe as it would be with our country without the protection of the dykes. It would be engulfed by the tide of sins like Holland by the flow of the waves."[7]

If she would accept this role in the church, then even though she would still suffer terribly, the pain would be counterbalanced by excessive joy. "Your vocation is clear; it consists in sacrificing yourself for others, in making reparation for faults you have not committed, in the practice of a sublime and truly divine charity... Say to Jesus: 'I wish to place myself of my own will upon your Cross, and I wish it to be you who drive in the nails.' Then she would see Mary and the Saints rejoicing."[8]

To meet Christ in her pain, she should meditate often on the cross. She should not think that Jesus suffered less because it was for a shorter amount of time, because having set aside his divinity Jesus experienced all the burden of all sin for all time.

In the course of many years of talking to other Catholics who are in physical pain, I have found that some readily accept the teaching the priest gave Lydwine, whereas others violently reject it. Those who are repulsed by the idea of victim-souls expiating for the sins of the world usually say that since Jesus already died for our sins, setting oneself up as an expiator is not only distorted but even blasphemous. Besides, since sinners have free will, given them by God, how can the sufferings of another change them? No matter how much grace is poured out on them, it appears that most of them continue on their evil way unchanged! If not even Jesus can change them, how could we do so by some sort of remote control of offering up our pain for them?

I myself used to fall in between the two groups: on the one hand, being happy to offer my occasional bouts of pain for sinners because it is better than thinking of it as useless agony; on the other, not really understanding how the spiritual exchange could work.

Last year, I heard an explanation that not only satisfied me but also explained the many passages in the lives of the saints about raining graces on others through self-offering. Christ honors our free will very highly. His general practice is to avoid overriding free will by overpowering graces. So touched is his heart, however, by the love of himself and of neighbor manifested when someone is willing to endure agonizing pain in expiation that this love is allowed to tip the scale, sending overpowering graces of contrition to the sinner!

Whether you agree with this spiritual theology or not, I am sure you will be happy to hear that soon after the visit of the priest, at Easter, right after receiving Holy Communion, Lydwine's soul was overwhelmed by love. She saw within herself the face of Christ in his passion.

Then she was full of joyful praise and instead of drowning in legitimate self-pity, she could only offer her sufferings to Christ. She wept with love for two weeks and she came not to envy her cheerful friends at play but instead to envy Veronica and Simon and Mary Magdalene. She began to complain that she was not suffering enough, thinking that by her suffering she was lessening those of Christ. She said that if recitation of one Hail Mary would free her from pain she would not say it.[9]

In fact, though, Lydwine's physcial pain became worse. Her stomach burst and she had to have a pillow pressed on her to keep her intestines from leaving her body. To move her they had to bind her together or her body would have fallen to pieces. She hardly ate at all in thirty years as much as another would eat in three days.

When asked if she wished to be healed, Lydwine would say, "No, there is but one thing now that I desire; it is not to be deprived of my discomforts and pains."[10] She didn't sleep at all.

Meanwhile, Lydwine was surrounded by curiosity seekers who refused to believe the stories about her continuing to live on without eating. They wanted to find a way to prove that she ate and drank at night in secret. They pestered her with questions. Others said she was possessed.

In 1421, the Burgomasters of Shiedam wrote a document to attest that she was genuine, that she did not eat or sleep, that her body was destroyed yet smelled of perfume. This was also attested to be true by six French soldiers, who had invaded Schiedam. Their curious commandant ordered them to watch Lydwine night and day to find out whether the stories about her miraculous life were true.

By then Lydwine had started asking in prayer for more pain to expiate particular sins.[11] The types of sins she would pick out to come against were the sins of carnival, of dying souls, of souls in purgatory. Her angel, whom she saw and conversed with perpetually, showed her the souls of bad priests so she would want to offer her sufferings for their conversion. She successfully interceded for her town against its imminent looting by enemy armies.

In the midst of all this suffering, Lydwine's soul was in ecstasy. During these ecstasies she would grind her teeth and twist herself and yet she would say that her consolations were so great that she would not change her pains for all the pleasures of life.[12]

Later God sent Lydwine a Franciscan priest who shared with her his love of God and belief in the meaning of suffering. Also God sent Lydwine a woman friend to tend her after the death of her mother.

The company of such holy people was most consoling since for so long the sufferer had to cope with a visiting priest who did not believe in her at all. He denied her Holy Communion on the main feasts since he thought her extraordinary mystical gifts came from the devil. Once he brought unconsecrated hosts to test her. She rejected these hosts immediately for Jesus had told her of the ruse.

For a short time God consoled Lydwine by coming to her in such power that all her pain left. An angel took away her wounds so that she looked like a healthy young woman. After this she saw Mary and the angels and then Jesus crucified who transpierced her feet, hands, and heart. The wounds were slightly covered over as she wished no one to see them.

After receiving these stigmata, Lydwine's former miseries returned. Though she was now ugly as ever, a white host on her breast remained from the visitation as a proof of the visit of the eucharistic Lord.[13]

During her last eight years of pain, Jesus sent her a holy priest to give her Communion often. He also sent many angels to keep her company. She said that these gave her the greatest joy because of their sublime beauty.[14]

Lydwine's guardian angel started to take her soul for walks to the parish church, to Eden, and to purgatory! On her walks through heaven, Lydwine would delight in the saints. In her ecstasies the saints would encourage her and tell her how all the torments would be over someday whereas her joy would be eternal.[15] In spite of these wonderful graces, Lydwine would cry at the thought of the many years she still had to live.

I imagine some readers are doubtful about Lydwine's out-of-body journeys. As proof, skeptics of her own time had to come to grips with inexplicable signs of the places she visited. From the Holy Land she returned with thorns from Calvary. Visitors to Holland from distant convents would be treated to intricate descriptions of the furnishing of their monasteries. Lydwine was also known for miraculous cures, predictions of the unlikely death of others to the hour, and exorcisms.

In spite of such closeness to God, our saint could experience piercing grief over human losses. At the time of the death of her father and her brother she believed that God took away her joy in him as a punishment for expressing so much grief for them instead of simply entrusting them to the Lord with expectancy of reunion in heaven.

I am sure some readers think that Lydwine's idea that God would withdraw because of the woman's natural attachment to loving kin is morbid, making God seem sadistic in his jealousy. I think there is room for another interpretation. When we are sunk in grief, we have no room in our hearts for consolations. In fact, we prefer to dwell in sadness as a sign of the degree of our love for the missing person. Once we begin to experience healing of grief, we are ready to make room for the joy of Christ's presence again.

After those deaths Lydwine was persecuted by ridiculing soldiers who came in the night and punched her until blood flowed.

In compensation God sent his beloved suffering sister a special blessing. There was a devastating fire in her town. The governors brought to her room for safekeeping the statue of the Virgin who had smiled at her when she was a child. The Virgin would tuck her in at night in her pain. In ecstasy Lydwine drank the milk of the Virgin at Christmas. Does such an image make you squeamish? Why not such sensory consolations for a woman racked by such sensory pains?

At the end of her life, Lydwine had new woes: epilepsy, apoplexy, sudden short madness. In a vision she saw that her body represented in microcosm all of what Europe was going through.[16]

Lydwine arranged that after her death her house would be a hospital for the destitute. At the end Jesus flooded her with delights and brought to her bedside Mary and the apostles, angels, and saints. Jesus himself anointed her.

When her body was laid out, Lydwine became as fair as she had been at seventeen. There was a smile on her face and all her ulcers and wounds were gone.[17] This transformation at death was also the case with the bodies of St. Francis of Assisi, St. Anthony, St. Lutgarde, Catherine of Siena, Catherine de Ricci, St. Madeleine dei Pazzi, and Rose of Lima.

People came in the millions to see her body laid out at the funeral. Many miracles occured during this time and after.

Who would want to deny to her the palm of being the greatest of all sufferers the church has known?

What have other saints who suffered greatly from physical pain and from exhaustion had to say about meeting Christ in their miseries?

I turn again to St. Bernard because he is a saint who wrote so eloquently about his own troubles. Bernard was often bedridden to the point that he expected to die of his ills. Ratisbonne writes about him: "Sickness is, to common souls, an occasion of weakness and slackness, which relaxes the springs of the spiritual life. To strong souls it is, on the contrary, an exercise of courage and patience, by means of which the Christian overcomes himself, tames his inferior nature, and learns to imitate the patience of Him who suffers for us—to leave us an example (1 Pt 2:21)."[18]

Though constantly in acute suffering and seemingly near death, St. Bernard was thronged by people in every country demanding healings, exorcisms, and diplomatic missions. In a letter to his monks back in Clairvaux telling them how much he longed to be with them instead of on one of these missions, he wrote:

At present the urgent solicitations of the emperor, the express command of the Pope, and the entreaties of the Church and the Christian princes, oblige me to go to Apulia, contrary to my inclination, all sick and languishing as I am, and bearing in my countenance the fearful token of approaching death... in all my labors and fatigues my only motive has been Him... who will one day repay me for all I have suffered for His sake. If I only serve him from necessity... I am an unfaithful servant; but if I serve him with all my heart, I shall give some glory.[19]

At fifty-four he was fragile and could hardly stand up. He was so emaciated that he seemed almost dead. Yet when called by the pope to preach the crusade, "he gradually became animated, and his sweet and burning words flowed from his lips, like a river of milk and honey, which sprang from his heart as from a furnace of divine love."[20]

After terrible apostolic labors, he repaired his strength in his cell at Clairvaux.

Earlier in our chapter on fear, we described how much St. Teresa of Avila suffered from illness and weariness. She was ordered to add to her other duties in the founding of convents and administration of her own, by writing an entire treatise on prayer to replace a book of hers which was being held up in the courts of the Inquisition.

Made miserable by tintinitus and dizziness, she took up her task resolutely, writing that "the strength given by obedience usually lessens the difficulty of things that seem impossible."[21]

Yet she admits that "if the pains are severe they then afflict the soul interiorly and exteriorly in such a way that it does not know what to do with itself; it would willingly accept at once martyrdom rather than sharp pains."[22]

John of the Cross had this stalwart method of coping with physical pain—to wish for them beforehand! He begged to die in a place where he would be not known and loved and in excruciating pain. Why? Because he wanted to be like Christ and because he knew that suffering is purifying.

God heard his prayer. At the end of his life, John suffered from inflammations and abscesses. He was forced to undergo operations where his legs were opened so that the nerves and bones were exposed from the heel to the top of the calf. He dictated a letter at the time to Dona Ana, a laywoman, who was his spiritual daughter, telling her of the great joy he experienced in suffering for the Lord.

Concerning the fatigue that comes with working too hard, John of the Cross used to recommend and practice the relief of solitude. He only slept two to three hours at night, but he used to flee to solitary grottos for restful communion with God. Still if called upon to carry the heavy load of administration, he would always obey.[23]

Most of the saints endured much physical pain. A listing in *The Treasury of Women Saints* of two hundred who survived a variety of difficulties shows physical suffering to be the most common.

For those living in the Southwest United States, the image of heroic endurance of pain that comes most quickly to mind is poor Blessed Junipero Serra, tramping up and down the coast lamed and in terrible pain, sometimes for relief pouring horse medicine into his wounded knee! Happy, of course, to have something big to offer to his beloved Saviour.

When St. Alphonsus Liguori was old, weakened by asthma, fever, and headaches, he vowed never to waste a moment of time. He wrote his famous *Meditations on the Passion* and this led to great peace.

St. Maximilian Kolbe did most of his apostolic work in conditions of chronic ill health. Once he collapsed from overwork and was hospitalized with serious tuberculosis for half a year. It is reported that "Father Maximilian always tried to keep it to himself if he was feeling bad so as not to discourage the rest of us. He always hid his sufferings that came from his poor health. Because he had only one lung he had difficulty breathing and this caused him to have tremendous headaches almost constantly, but you never heard it from him. He never complained. On the other hand, if one of us got sick, he would stay with him twenty-four hours if necessary to see he got every possible attention."[24]

When on a mission in Japan the Franciscans of the Immaculata lived in conditions of poverty. Kolbe's tuberculosis persisted alarmingly. He had high fevers, chills, and shakes. His doctor advised him to enter a sanatorium but he refused saying that it would not cure him, and he would rather work as long as he could. One night he thought he was dying since his pulse was getting weaker and weaker. He told one of the brothers that if he died during the night it should be told that his last advice was "Stick close to the Blessed Mother."[25] He recovered. One of his doctors reported that although he was frail he was prudent about his health, neither irresponsible nor exaggeratedly concerned.

During this time he wrote in a letter to his community in Poland, "I am scared of suffering and the thought of calamities... but even Jesus in the Garden of Gethsemane was afraid. This comforts me...."[26] When too sick to get up, he would teach and write letters from the bed.

Of course, the conditions in the concentration camp at Auschwitz would be most difficult for one so weak to begin with. Kolbe surprised everyone with his serene manner and by his joy in God, enabling him to get the trainload of prisoners on the way to the feared camp to sing with him. The first morning the prisoners were taken for icy showers. They had to eat and drink only some poorly contrived coffee, watery soup, bread, and a small piece of sausage on special occasions such as the birthday of Hitler! They slept on straw. He would be assigned manual labor too much for his strength, but if another prisoner tried to help him wheel his barrow they were both beaten. All such trials he would teach the others to offer up to God.[27]

Eventually, after being beaten mercilessly by one of the many Nazis who hated priests, he was dragged to the hospital, totally exhausted and depleted, but still saying that "for Jesus Christ I'm ready to suffer more than this. The Immaculata is helping me." He would refuse any help his devoted followers offered that others would not receive. When he could have left the ward, he wanted to stay to continue to give hope to the dying, giving them absolution, pressing them to his chest like a mother to comfort them, telling them, "Take Christ's hand in one of yours and Mary's in the other. Now even if you are in darkness you can go forward with the confidence of a child guided by its parents."[28]

STEPS TO MEETING CHRIST IN THE SUFFERINGS OF PAIN AND FATIGUE

1. We should always begin by praying for healing in the case of illness and pain and for relief in the case of exhausting labors.

2. We should not be alarmed if we reject suffering; even Lydwine did for many years. Lydwine cried over her miseries. False bravado brings no comfort.

3. If there is no relief for our suffering, we must unite each moment of it with the pain of Jesus. It is important to realize that during his passion, he felt the suffering of all of humanity throughout all ages. We are not alone. He is suffering with us.

4. Ask Jesus to send visions of your destiny in heaven, so you can bear your pain better.

TWELVE

Meeting Christ in the Suffering of Temptation

Then Jesus was led up by the Spirit into the wilderness to be tempted by the devil. Matthew 4:1

And to keep me from being too elated by the abundance of revelations, a thorn was given me in the flesh, a messenger of Satan, to harass me, to keep me from being too elated. Three times I besought the Lord about this, that it should leave me; but he said to me, "My grace is sufficient for you, for my power is made perfect in weakness." 2 Corinthians 12:7-9

We wonder sometimes. With all the pain and misery from so many natural sufferings, why does God also subject us to a battle with forces greater than ourselves? How can a puny, weak human being be victorious against powerful demons, wily devils, satanic attacks?

In books about the nature of demonic activity we can read about demonic temptations going all the way from oppression to full-scale possession. And yet we are also taught in Catholic theology that God will never let the devil have the victory over us if we persevere in prayer, trusting that our guardian angel, the entire angelic host, and his gracious love are more than equal to any works of the evil one.

In Scripture we have one explanation for why God allows demonic attacks on his beloved children. In the book of Job, we are told that God gives Satan this power because he wants to test and demonstrate the heroic virtue and love of his precious saint.

In the life of Jesus, there can be no question at all of God testing his Son to see how good he will be since he is all good and free from all sin. Yet the famous forty days in the desert are given as a sort of icon to us that we may realize in what ways Satan likes to tempt us, and how to come against those glamorous-sounding false promises.

In the famous passage about St. Paul's thorn in the flesh, we find a model for temptation of Christian saints, for the emphasis is on the danger to pride that comes with astounding supernatural graces. God averts this danger by leaving in the saints humiliating temptations to sin that burst aflame under the provocations of Satan. When we read about how the saints came against these assaults, we take courage for ourselves.

Since temptation to sexual sin is the most common and humiliating, I will concentrate on it in this chapter, but the same pattern can be found in temptations to violence or even to malicious conversation. In every case the devil tries to make it seem as if the sinner will attain infinite bliss or tremendous relief by giving way to impulses that seem overpowering: "Engage in this illicit sexual act, even just once, and you will be ecstatic. If you resist, you will fall into a sadness and desolation that will never leave you.

"Kill your enemy or the person who betrayed you. Even if you have to go to jail or be executed, it would be worth it to finally see him or her crushed forever.

"Tell as many people as possible about the faults of your opponent. Why should they retain a good opinion of him or her? Let that enemy suffer as much as he or she makes you suffer every day. How superior you will feel when everyone knows!"

How did the saints come against such compelling lies?

ST. CATHERINE OF SIENA: TEMPTED BUT UNVANQUISHED

The saint I have chosen as our "star" may surprise you. Catherine was one of the most angelic of all creatures, never having even a venial sin to confess. Yet God allowed her to experience some of the worst temptations against purity of any saint.

I am choosing Catherine just because of her purity, for many Christians allow the devil to deceive them into thinking that if they could even entertain evil impulses, it is proof that they are utterly shameful and can never be transformed in Christ into holiness. If Catherine went through such miseries, why can't we?

Now let us read about the life and temptations of St. Catherine of Siena, the fourteenth-century Third Order Dominican Doctor of the Church.

The best biography of Catherine is by Blessed Raymond of Capua, her confessor and spiritual son.[1] I do not think any biography can be as vivid as a good one written by an eyewitness. Who but a beloved friend would say that even though Catherine was a most wonderful Catholic saint, she was nothing much to look at. Eventually, when she hardly ate at all, she seemed to be but a bag of bones!

Catherine was born in 1347 to a family of dyers. She was the twenty-fourth child of her fertile mother and father. Her twin sister died shortly after the birth, causing such sorrow that the couple quickly produced another as a replacement! It is exciting to think that one of the most famous women of all times would have so little chance of being born in our contraceptive society.

Little Caterina was so charming and wise that even though she was never especially pretty, she was always sought after. At the age of six, God gave her a grace so stupendous that it framed the rest of her life. Running an errand with her older brother, the child paused for a moment to glance across the valley.

There in the sky above the roof of the church of the Friars Preachers, she saw the vision of a splendid audience-hall, furnished like a royal court. Within it was the Savior of the world... with him were Peter and Paul and John the Evangelist. Entranced and rooted to the spot, she fixed her eyes on the sight... [He] smiled on her with surpassing affection, stretched out his hand over her and made the Sign of the Cross... she was transported out of herself... she lost all consciousness... Stefano (her brother) called out to her two or three times to attract her attention... like a person awaking from a heavy sleep she said "Oh, if you but saw what I am looking at, you would never try to take me away from a sight so delightful."[2]

The vision led Catherine to withdraw from the family hubbub to be alone in prayer. She was seen to levitate off the ground. At seven she made a vow of consecration to Christ. The family was not delighted by these strange events. They had been hoping to make a good match for her, one beneficial to the finances of the clan.

They tried to convince her to adorn herself more attractively. She gave in for a short while and let her older sister fix her up while inwardly swearing to be true to her vow. For this compromise she would berate herself mercilessly in later years.

When her parents brought the young girl into society to meet potential mates, Catherine would flee from the room. Furious, they brought her to a Dominican confessor, sure that he would insist on obedience. Instead Catherine convinced the priest of her vocation, and he advised her to chop off her long hair as a proof of her commitment to be a bride of Christ alone.

Desperate, her parents punished Catherine by exiling her from the little cell she liked to pray in and insisting instead that she be the family cook and maid. They thought this might show her that it would be better to be married to a rich man than to persist in rebellion.

In response, our stubborn saint took on her new tasks joyfully, singing hymns all day, making of her heart the cell where she could meet her beloved Lord. One day seeing a holy dove above the head of his daughter, Catherine's father gave up, saying, "We can never make a match for her which can be compared to this. We need not think we are the losers if we receive into our home not a mortal man, but him who is immortal, God and man."[3]

Now begins a period of alarming penitential practices. Subject to stomach disorders from an early age, Catherine now took to eating less and less, mostly a little bread and raw vegetables, and by her twentieth year only raw vegetables. Yet her skin remained pliant and her face shining. She slept on wooden planks and wore a chain, flagellated herself, and slept only a half hour or so every three days.[4]

Catherine carried on a perpetual conversation with Christ, and could talk about him for days on end if anyone would listen. Her famous tome, *The Dialogue*, was dictated to several scribes at once. Illiterate, but wanting to read the Breviary, Jesus himself taught her how to read and recited it with her.

The great desire of Catherine at this time was to be able to join the Third Order Dominican women called the Mantellate. They were hesitant, for since they went about in the streets doing works of mercy, they chose only older women. A younger woman might cause scandal. Catherine prayed and prayed to be admitted. This came about when she developed such an incredibly ugly case of chronic acne that no could think she would attract sinful attention!

Now comes the long battle of Catherine with the temptations of Satan. Here are some excerpts from Blessed Raymond's description:[5]

The Ancient Serpent was now clearly aware that this girl had begun to scale the summits of perfection. He grew afraid that she would achieve salvation not only for herself but for many other souls as well; that she would, by her merits and her doctrine, be a bulwark of the holy city, the Catholic Church.

So he bent the whole strength of his spiritual wickedness, and all his thousand arts, to the task of seducing her from her vocation. But the God of all mercy was allowing this to happen, only to make her crown the brighter... He moved her by an inward inspiration to pray to him for the virtue of courage, and she did so unceasingly for many days....

[Jesus told her]: "Daughter, in order to obtain the virtue of courage you must follow my own example. By my divine power I could have annihilated all the forces which assailed me... to show men an example to follow, I chose to overthrow my enemies by no other way than that of the cross... with its load of shame and suffering... For my sake, then, daughter, accept once for all, all sweet things as bitter, and all bitter things as sweet; and then, come what may, lay aside all misgivings; you will have the strength to endure without flinching whatever comes."

First come temptations of the flesh. Not satisfied with putting these thoughts into her mind, and filling her fancy with seductive images as she slept, they forced them on her outward senses also, alluring her eyes and ears with a thousand shapes and sounds, in bodies they have fashioned for themselves out of thin air...

With unflinching courage she stands up against Self—against her very flesh and blood. With her iron chain she scourges her body till the blood flows... [Voices tell her all day] "Do you imagine you can keep them [her penances] for ever? Impossible! unless you want to kill yourself and end up as a suicide. Be wise in time... It is not yet too late to enjoy the delights which life can offer... Live the life that other women do. Take a husband. Be a mother of children... Have not saintly women been wives and mothers... "

To this she would reply: "I rely upon our Lord Jesus Christ, and not upon myself." No other word than this could they draw from her; she kept on steadfastly at her prayers.

Later in her life, in conversation with us, her disciples, she would lay down for us as a rule of action that, when troubled by temptation we must never enter into argument with the Enemy... "A wife who is faithful to her husband should give no answer to one who tempts her to infidelity, but just keep away from him as best she can... Faith is the virtue which conquers every temptation."

Faced with this, he [Satan] changed his tactics. He now began to conjure up pictures of men and women of licentious conduct who seemed to posture lasciviously before her, filling her eyes with obscene sights and her ears with filthy language, and calling on her with frenzied cries to join in their orgies...

She told me that at that time, turn her eyes where she would in her cell, she saw it so swarming with demons and with incitements to evil thoughts, that she was impelled to run from it in order to escape from them, if only for a time. As a result she now came to spend more time in church than before....

Then one day, a long time after these trials had begun, she came back from church and bowed down in prayer. At once a ray of brightness from the Holy Spirit shone upon her and flooded her mind with light... [she replied to the devil's boast that he would never leave her] "I have made choice of suffering as the well-spring of my strength. It is no hardship for me, but rather a delight, to endure for my Saviour's name all you have been inflicting on me, and more besides, for as long as it shall please his Majesty."

At these words the demon horde turned tail and fled pellmell, and a great light from heaven flooded the little room. And there, at the heart of the brightness, was our Lord Jesus Christ himself, nailed upon the cross and covered with his blood... From that cross he spoke to her these words: "My daughter Catherine, look at what I have suffered for your sake. Do not take it hard, then, when you too must suffer something for my sake."

And where were you, Lord, while my heart was suffering the agony of all those horrors? And our Lord said: "I was in your heart.... When the struggle had reached the point I had fixed beforehand I sent forth my light, and the Powers of Darkness turned tail and fled. They cannot face the Light... It was when you did offer yourself without reserve to undergo them [the temptations] that in a flash I revealed my presence and came to your rescue. For what I take pleasure in is not sufferings in themselves, but the generosity that accepts them as love of me."[5]

After this, Jesus spent more and more time talking to Catherine intimately and drawing her into the mystical marriage. She would go on to a life full of miraculous ministry to others: to townspeople, to sinful priests, to bishops, kings, and popes.

Yet at the end of her life as she lay close to death, she was besieged by demonic violence, which she accepted in the same valiant humble manner. She offered these physical lashings of Satan that Christ's justice might be overwhelmed by his mercy for the sake of the church then so ruined by schism and sin. In this way she taught her disciples and we, her readers, not to be afraid of anything!

I strongly advise those who are fearful of demonic temptations to read her biography and her own *Dialogue*,[6] for she is one of the best saints for bringing courage to tormented souls.

From *The Dialogue* here is some advice about temptations (that Catherine heard from the mouth of Christ in locutions):

We should not think that when consolations and visions are withdrawn to be replaced by temptations that Christ has left us. He makes this happen to keep us from being spiritually selfish, so that we might change from being weak beings to being strong saints attached to Truth.[7]

The devil fears hearts on fire with love of God.[8]

If the soul has the least bit of knowledge and heat and hatred of sin, she resists him [Satan], binding her will steadfast with the chains of hatred for sin and love for virtue.[9]

[Those in true union with God] are always peaceful and calm, and nothing can scandalize them because they have done away with what causes them to take scandal, their self-will. They trample underfoot all the persecutions the world and the devil can hound them with. They can stand in water of great troubles and temptations, but it cannot hurt them because they are anchored to the vine of burning desire... They find joy in everything.[10]

I have appointed the demons to tempt and trouble my creatures in this life. Not that I want my creatures to be conquered, but I want them to conquer and receive from me the glory of victory when they have proved their virtue. No one need fear any battle or temptation of the devil that may come, for I have made you strong and given your wills power in the blood of my Son.

Neither the devil nor any other creature can change this will of yours, for it is yours, given by me with the power of free choice. You, then, can hold or lose it as you please, by your free choice... if you refuse to put this weapon, your will, into the devil's hands, that is, if you refuse to consent to his tempting and troubling you will never be hurt in any temptation by the guilt of sin. Indeed, temptation will strengthen you, provided you open your mind's eye to see my charity, which lets you be tempted only to bring you to virtue and to prove your virtue.[11]

When we search through the history of Christian sanctity looking for instances of overcoming temptation, we want to pause for the heroic battles of the Desert Fathers, depicted so vividly in famous paintings such as that of Grunewald of the aged St. Anthony surrounded by gruesome tormenting demons.

But before tapping the wisdom they transmitted from such spiritual warfare, it is interesting to read the mystics reporting that the Virgin Mary also was tempted by Satan: "Irritated by her perfect virtue and holiness, the devil vainly attempted to incite her to commit even a slight venial sin... she suffered from the strain and wept... without once losing her inner union with God... she conquered all these temptations."[12]

The same mystics report that during renewed attacks of Satan, Mary would respond by quoting Scriptural truth, singing hymns, and by recommitting to suffering for the sake of sinners.[13]

It is said that after the early persecutions, there was so much laxity in the church that those who wanted to lead lives dedicated to gospel truth were attracted to the desert to live as hermits. Free from the temptations of the world, these ascetical-minded monks would instead be assailed directly by

Satan. Their sayings about how to deal with temptation were then transmitted to younger desert monks and to Christians in the world looking for realistic advice from veteran spiritual warriors.

Here are some of the sayings of the early Fathers of the Church:[14]

When sin is understood by the soul, it is hated by it like a foul-smelling beast. But when it is not understood, it is loved by him who does not understand it and, enslaving its lover, keeps him in captivity. And the poor miserable man does not see what can save him, and does not even think about it; but thinking that sin adorns him, he welcomes it gladly.

St. Anthony the Great

In thy strife with the devil thou hast for spectators the Angels and the Lord of Angels. St. Ephraem

Evil thought, for those who cast it down in themselves, is a sign of their love of God and not of sin; for not the impact of the thought is sin, but friendly converse of the mind with it. If we have no fondness of it, why do we linger in it? It is impossible that anything we hate wholeheartedly should have long converse with our heart, unless we are wickedly parties to it. St. Mark and Ascetic

As the pilot of a vessel is tried in a storm; as the wrestler is tried in the ring; the soldier in the battle, and the hero in adversity: so is the Christian tried in temptation. St. Basil

As soon as lust assails us, let us instantly say: "Lord, assist me, do not permit me to offend you." St. Jerome

And why, it is asked, are there so many snares? That we may not fly low, but seek the things that are above.

St. John Chrysostom

When the sly demon, after using many devices, fails to hinder the prayer of the diligent, he desists a little; but when the man has finished his prayer, he takes his revenge. He either fires his anger and thus destroys the fair state produced by prayer, or excites an impulse toward some animal pleasure and thus mocks his mind. St. Nilus of Sinai

Do not oppose the thoughts, which the enemy sows in you, but rather cut off all converse with them by prayer to God.

St. Isaak of Syria

St. Benedict advised that "when evil thoughts come into one's heart, it is best to dash them at once on the rock of Christ and to manifest them to one's spiritual father."[15]

In the early days of his life as a hermit, when tempted to return to the world "he threw himself into a nearby thicket of brambles and nettles." In this rule for monks, he advised to come against temptations of the flesh by "chastising the body and not seeking after soft living."[16]

Benedict's monks were only allowed to live as hermits if they were "strong enough for single combat with the devil."[17]

Another spiritual master, St. John Climacus wrote: "Let us rush with joy and trepidation to the noble contest and with no fear of our enemies [the devils]. If they see our spirits cowering and trembling, they will make a more vigorous attack against us. They hesitate to grapple with a bold fighter."[18]

St. Bernard tempted by sensuality as a young man flung himself into an icy pond. He also found relief in meditating on the sufferings of Christ. The reason he thought such remedies helpful was because he thought that sensuality was a way to find oblivion from our sufferings. If we rush toward suffering, then we turn away from the escape of sensuality.[19]

When tempted to stop preaching because he noticed how vain he was becoming of his speaking abilities, St. Bernard exclaimed, "Go away, Satan. I did not begin for you and I shall not stop for you."

In reading the lives of the saints, we find that many are freed from sexual temptation by praying to Mary. After a vision of the Blessed Virgin, as you recall, St. Ignatius was free all her life in thought and deed.[20]

St. Teresa of Avila who had great temptations to chat in the parlor instead of spending longer times in contemplative prayer in the chapel, suggests that with all temptations it is particularly important to avoid occasions of sin.[21] This old-fashioned concept is now made fun of by some Catholics, but it seems to me eminently reasonable. How can someone expect to give up talking too much in a gossipy way to friends if you make plans to visit such people for long periods of time? Or how avoid temptations to smoking if you keep the cigarettes nearby?

In general, St. Teresa taught that since we cannot exist in a fixed state of absorption in prayer, temptations are inevitable. They help us to see our own nothingness. When afflicted, we can only wait on God's mercy.

St. John of the Cross was an exorcist. Himself persecuted by apparitions and blows of demons, he recommended fasting and prayer.[22]

Our old friend, St. Martin de Porres, of our chapter on empathy, was subject to terrible demonic assaults.[23] A soldier who was visiting the Dominican monastery was staying in the same cell as Martin. He heard Martin yelling at someone and was surprised since Martin was so kind that he never raised his voice.

"I didn't see anybody with him, but I saw that he was being rolled around the cell, and I could hear blows struck. Many blows... All at once I noticed that a fire was burning in the clothes Brother Martin had heaped up for the sick... When we had put out the fire, Brother Martin told me not to be afraid... " When he woke up there was no sign of the fire and the soldier realized that it had been a manifestation of the devil.

Blessed Marie of the Incarnation went through terrible temptations to blasphemy, immodesty, and suicide. These periods were compounded by migraine headaches and feelings of extreme annoyance with her companions.[24] This lasted for two years.

She persevered out of faith that God was hidden within her. She would keep up her vocal prayer regardless of how sad she would become, and always ask for the intercession of Mary. If she saw the devil mocking her, she would make the sign of the cross, and then she would feel interior peace and sweetness even while the temptations continued. During this time she was much helped by her Jesuit director.

Matt Talbot, a former alcoholic, suffered from violent oppression by demons as soon as he had made up his mind to stay sober.[25]

Once he was waiting for early morning Mass outside the church when he felt himself violently pushed back two times as he was trying to go in to Mass. He responded by invoking the names of Jesus and Mary and then he could walk in.

Another time, he was walking up to the altar rail and suddenly felt a wave of absolute despair and certainty he would go back to drinking. He walked out of the church and wandered around Dublin until he came to another church. Again came the despair, and again he left the church. Then he prostrated himself in public in front of the church and stretched out his arms in the form of a cross, praying aloud to Mary and Jesus to be delivered from temptation. The despair left and he joyfully went into the church.

In the long run, in trying to overcome temptation to drink Talbot realized that he had to overcome the cravings of his body.

This he did by fasting and penances, all the more admirable since such practices are usually associated with monastic life where one is surrounded by a conducive atmosphere and the helpful companionship of the others. But Matt did his penances in his tenement house and on his construction job without any friendly supporters.

Talbot wanted to suffer in atonement for the blasphemies and other sins of his life when he was drunk. To recall his resolution he put two pins on his coat sleeve in the form of a cross. He became a contemplative praying on Sunday for six to seven hours on his knees in church. He fasted often and slept on planks. He also wore chains around his body inside his clothing. In this way he would feel close to Christ on the cross.

Talbot was especially close to Mary who he would talk to during the night. He also was devoted to following the passion of Christ by making the stations of the cross.

After his father died, his mother lived with him and heard him talking to Mary by the hour, carrying a statue of the Virgin and Child into bed on his planks where he only slept two to three hours. He tipped his hat whenever someone said the name of Jesus in vain. He was ridiculed on the docks because of this practice. Once a group of workers got used to this seemingly eccentric comrade, new employees would come along who didn't know who he was and would ridicule him.

Later, he joined the Third Order of St. Francis and prayed the fifteen-decade rosary and many other litanies.

Conchita (Concepcion Cabrera de Armida), the Mexican saint of our century who suffered so deeply at the death of her son, a daughter, and her beloved husband, was a spiritual guide to many priests, nuns, and lay people concerning interior trials. She believed that praying before the Blessed Sacrament was a decisive remedy for coping with temptations. Here is a meditation she suggested concerning meeting Christ in the suffering of temptation.

The tempest rages in the bottom of my soul. Storms succeed storms unceasingly, the bitter waters of suffering come to my lips and have inundated my heart.

I feel lost, my Jesus, in the midst of these rising floods, floods of pride, anger and jealousy, envy and spite! Save me, Jesus, awake and listen to me or I perish!...

Flattery in some form is a necessity for me. I let myself be guided by my nerves and by passing impressions which leave my heart cold and void...

Calm, then, the hurricane which threatens to shipwreck me and the tempest which is ready to engulf me!

Calm my temptations; dissipate these black clouds which are about to burst over my head, my Jesus, and save me!

O Mary, star of the sea, pacify the heaven of my soul and say to my Jesus, "Save him, save him, for he is my child and he is about to perish!"[26]

STEPS IN TURNING TO CHRIST IN THE SUFFERINGS OF TEMPTATION

1. When afflicted with demonic temptations, it is absolutely necessary to seek spiritual direction, and if advised, deliverance prayer.

2. Under siege we need to call out to Christ for protection, asking also for special graces of aid from Mary, the saints, our guardian angel, and the other angels.

3. The use of sacramentals such as holy water and relics can also be helpful.

4. In cases of annoyance caused by demonic suggestion it is never good to argue with Satan. Rather than allowing one-

self to get too upset, it is better to try to ignore the evil images and ideas being thrust upon the soul in temptation, and even to laugh at them with the confidence of the Lord.

THIRTEEN

Joy in the Midst of Suffering

As for the saints in the land, they are the noble, in whom is all my delight. Psalm 16:3

Indeed as the sufferings of Christ overflow to us, so, through Christ, does our consolation overflow. 2 Corinthians 1:3-5

The saints were bold players who staked their all on a chessboard where what is won is won forever. What they have won is peace. Their radiance tells us so.

Anges de la Groce, *St. Benedict Joseph Labre*

Coming to the end of our long exploration of how to meet Christ in suffering in the spirit of the saints, we wonder. We see how they experienced pain as "the kiss from the cross," but we are not so sure how we are to do it. Our minds range over the many miseries in our lives: addiction, confrontation with error, doubt, empathy, exploitation, failure, poverty, fear, frustration, despair, physical pain, loneliness, marital discord, persecution, temptation. Will we ever emerge victorious and happy from all these trials?

After my own spiritual journey in the writing of *The Kiss from the Cross*, I find hope and joy in these truths gleaned from the lives of my saints:

- Whereas in fairy tales all the difficulties come first, then the hero and heroine marry, and they live happily ever after with death never mentioned; in the story of the saints being drawn closer to Christ first comes many years of intense suffering with intense joy in the spiritual marriage, interior peace in the depths of the soul, and a promise of eternal bliss.

- All the energy I put into running away from pain, the saints put into running toward Christ. As a result, when I want to find joy in Christ I have to retrace my steps, whereas they dwell in possession of their beloved, finding joy in him in the midst of their trials.

- In their union with Christ, the saints did not suffer alone. Their suffering was his and his theirs. Everything for them was more intimate, if inescapable. I can imitate them by longing for that intimacy instead of escaping into my addictions.

- While I cannot force myself through sheer willpower to drum up suffering for Christ, I should desire to offer up sufferings in my life for him. Such a desire for suffering, which then has real redemptive value, is *not* morbid. I need to give more time to prayer, asking Jesus to inundate me with love, so that I will become stronger. In the meantime weak as I am, by humble acceptance of pain that cannot be evaded, I can prepare myself for closer union with its greater solace.

- I must not shrink from the realization that I need purification in pain to be purged of my sins and imperfections.

- In my love for the church and all people created by God, I need to stop myself from sinking in self-pity. I need to ask the Holy Spirit to remind me that I can offer my sufferings for others believing that Christ will use those offerings to build his kingdom. I shall remember that Jesus took joy in the cross wanting in his love to redeem us, to open the doors of eternal happiness for us.

• In the end, what choice do we have? To suffer joylessly in distraction or despair, or, like the saints, to rejoice in the midst of suffering, trusting in the promises of him who went to terrible lengths to prove his promises were real?

"Rejoice in the Lord always; again I will say rejoice."

Philippians 4:4

Notes

INTRODUCTION
Meeting Christ in Suffering in the Spirit of the Saints

1. From the Office of Readings August 23, 1342.
2. Toni Morrison, *Sula* (New York: Plume-Penguin, 1982), 66.
3. Paul Scott, *The Raj Quartet* (New York: William Morrow & Company, 1976), 305.

ONE
Meeting Christ in the Suffering of Doubt

1. Cindy Cavnar, *Prayers and Meditations of Thérèse of Lisieux* (Ann Arbor, Mich.: Servant, 1993), 75.
2. Cavnar, 76.
3. Ida Goerres, *The Hidden Face: A Study of St. Thérèse of Lisieux*, translated by Richard and Clara Winston (New York: Pantheon, 1959), 357.
4. Goerres, 374-375.
5. Cavnar, 72.
6. Goerres, 360.
7. Cavnar, 73.
8. Raphael Brown, *The Life of Mary as Seen by the Mystics* (Milwaukee: The Bruce Publishing Company, 1951), 173.
9. Chervin, *Quotable Saints* (Ann Arbor, Mich.: Servant, 1992), 85.
10. Chervin, *Quotable Saints*, 86.
11. St. John of the Cross, *Collected Works*, translated by Kieran Kavanaugh, O.C.D., and Otilio Rodriguez, O.C.D. (Washington, D.C.: ICS Publications, 1979), 119ff.
12. Federico Ruiz, O.C.D., Project Director *God Speaks in the Night: The Life, Times and Teaching of St. John of the Cross*, translated by Kieran Kavanaugh, O.C.D. (Washington, D.C.: ICS, 1991), 313.
13. *Francis de Sales, Jane de Chantal, Letters of Spiritual Direction*, translated by Peronne Marie Thibert, V.H.M. (New York: Paulist Press, 1988), 78, 153-154.

14. Leon von Matt and Dom Hilpisch, O.S.B., *Saint Benedict*, translated by Dom Ernest Graf, O.S.B. (Chicago: Henry Regnery, 1961), 114.

15. Henri Joly, *Saint Ignatius of Loyola*, translated by Mildred Patridge (London: Duckworth and Company, 1899), 5.

16. Joly, 15-16.

17. Joly, 37ff.

18. Joly, 44.

19. Joly, 45.

20. Joly, 47.

21. Joly, 102-103.

22. Joly, 114.

23. Joly, 162.

24. Joly, 226.

25. Joly, 123-130.

26. Francois Charmot, S.J., *Ignatius Loyola and Francis de Sales* (St. Louis: B. Herder, 1966).

27. Joly, 16.

28. John Henry Cardinal Newman, *Apologia Pro Vita Sua* (New York: Modern Library, 1950).

29. Newman, 210.

30. From *Meditations and Devotions* quoted in *The Heart of Newman* edited by Erich Przywara, S.J. (Springfield, Ill.: Templegate, 1963), 42.

TWO
Meeting Christ in the Suffering of Being Exploited

1. Fr. Martin-Maria Olive, O.P. *Praxedes: Wife, Mother, Widow and Lay Dominican*, translated by Sister Maria Maez, O.P. (Rockford, Ill.: Tan, 1980), 10.

2 .Olive, 33.

3. Olive, 47.

4. Olive, 63.

5. Olive, 72.

6. Olive, 138.

7. Olive, 162.

8. St. Teresa of Avila, *The Interior Castle*, Vol. II of *The Collected Works*, (Washington, D.C.: I.C.S., 1980).

9. See Teresa Advices #25 quoted in Olive, 94.

10. Olive, 94 from *Foundations* of Teresa of Avila, 5, #8.

11. Dana Black, "Germaine of Pibrac" *Woman to Woman*, by Ronda Chervin and Terri Vorndan Nichols (San Francisco: Ignatius Press, 1990).

12. *Butler's Lives of the Saints*, edited, revised, and supplemented by Herbert J. Thurston, S.J. and Donald Attwater in 4 volumes, (Westminster, Md.: Christian Classics, 1981), Vol. III, 519-524.

13. *Butler's Lives of the Saints*, Vol. III, 524.

THREE
Meeting Christ In the Suffering of Failure and Poverty

1. Agnes De La Gorce, *Saint Benedict Joseph Labre*, translated by Rosemary Sheed (New York: Sheed and Ward, 1952).
2. De La Gorce, 3.
3. De La Gorce, 12.
4. De La Gorce, 34.
5. De La Gorce, 39.
6. De La Gorce, 50.
7. De La Gorce, 52.
8. De La Gorce, 72.
9. De La Gorce, 74.
10. De La Gorce, 81.
11. von Matt and Hilpisch, 8.
12. von Matt and Hilpisch, 76.
13. von Matt and Hilpisch, 91.
14. von Matt and Hilpisch, 137.
15. Ratisbonne, *The Life and Times of Saint Bernard* (N.Y.: Sadlier, 1865), 453 ff.
16. Ratisbonne, *Saint Bernard of Clairvaux* (Rockford, Ill.: Tan Books, 1991), 411ff.
17. Ratisbonne, 421.
18. Ratisbonne, 417.
19. Ronda De Sola Chervin, *Treasury of Women Saints* (Ann Arbor, Mich.: Servant, 1992), 62-64.
20. Fr. Bruno, O.D.C., *Saint John of the Cross*, (London: Sheed and Ward, 1936), 320.
21. Fr. Bruno, 321.
22. Fr. Bruno, 328.
23. Fr. Bruno, 325.
24. Adrian L. van Kaam, C.S.Sp., *A Light to the Gentiles: The Life-Story of the Venerable Francis Libermann*, (Pittsburgh: Duquesne University, 1959).
25. Chervin, *Quotable Saints*, 50.

FOUR
Meeting Christ in the Suffering of Fear

1. Adrian L. van Kaam, C.S.Sp.
2. van Kaam, 1.
3. van Kaam, 2.
4. van Kaam, 5.
5. van Kaam, 25.
6. van Kaam, 27.
7. van Kaam, 38.
8. van Kaam, 44.
9. van Kaam, 49.

10. van Kaam, 31.
11. van Kaam, 39.
12. St. Teresa of Avila, 362.
13. St. Teresa of Avila, 312.
14. Chervin, *Quotable Saints*, 100.
15. Chervin, *Quotable Saints*, 100.
16. Chervin, *Quotable Saints*, 100.
17. Chervin, *Quotable Saints*, 101.
18. Chervin, *Quotable Saints*, 101.
19. St. Teresa of Avila, 440.
20. Chervin, *Quotable Saints*, 100.
21. Charmot, 67.
22. Charmot, 84.
23. Chervin, *Quotable Saints*, 101.

FIVE
Meeting Christ in the Suffering of Frustration

1. Helene Magaret, *A Kingdom and a Cross: St. Alphonsus Liguori* (Milwaukee: The Bruce Publishing Co., 1958).
2. Magaret, 33.
3. Magaret, 80.
4. Magaret, 200ff.
5. Magaret, 196.
6. Magaret, 204.
7. Magaret, 209.
8. St. Alphonsus de Liguori, *The Sermons of St. Alphonsus Liguori* (Rockford, Ill.: Tan, 1982).
9. These quotations are all taken from St. Alphonsus de Liguori, *The Sermons of St. Alphonsus Liguori*, 254-262.
10. Chervin, *Quotable Saints*, 16-17.
11. Ratisbonne, 160ff.
12. Ratisbonne, 234.
13. Ratisbonne, 348.
14. Chervin, *Quotable Saints*, 18.
15. St. Teresa of Avila, 449.
16. Fr. Bruno, 146.
17. Fr. Bruno, 154.
18. Fr. Bruno, 198.
19. Chervin, *Quotable Saints*, 19.
20. Chervin, *Quotable Saints*, 19.

SIX
Meeting Christ in the Suffering of Interior Trials

1. *The Life and Sayings of Saint Catherine of Genoa*, translated and edited by Paul Garvin (Staten Island: Alba House, 1964).
2. *The Life and Sayings of Saint Catherine of Genoa*, 23.
3. *The Life and Sayings of Saint Catherine of Genoa*, 24-25.
4. *The Life and Sayings of Saint Catherine of Genoa*, 27.
5. *The Life and Sayings of Saint Catherine of Genoa*, 41-42.
6. *The Life and Sayings of Saint Catherine of Genoa*, 50.
7. *The Life and Sayings of Saint Catherine of Genoa*, 91.
8. *The Life and Sayings of Saint Catherine of Genoa*, 68.
9. St. Teresa of Avila, 344.
10. Fr. Bruno, 308.
11. Cindy Cavnar, 78.
12. St. Teresa of Avila, 301.
13. Charmot, 62-63.
14. Cavnar, 113.
15. Cavnar, 114.
16. Cavnar, 77.
17. Brown, 67.
18. St. Teresa of Avila, 440.
19. St. John of the Cross, 410-411.
20. Joly, 30.
21. St. Teresa of Avila, 301-302.
22. St. Teresa of Avila, 363ff.
23. St. Teresa of Avila, 305.
24. Fr. Bruno, 224.
25. John Edward Beahn, *A Man Born Again: Saint Thomas More* (Milwaukee: The Bruce Publishing Company, 1954), 95.
26. *Marie of the Incarnation: Selected Writings*, edited by Irene Mahoney, O.S.U. (New York: Paulist Press, 1989).
27. *Marie of the Incarnation*, 149ff.
28. *Marie of the Incarnation*, 149ff.
29. *Marie of the Incarnation*, 275-276.
30. De La Gorce, 72.
31. Mary Neill and Ronda Chervin, *Great Saints, Great Friends*, (Staten Island: Alba House, 1990), 136.
32. Paul Scott, *The Raj Quartet*, (New York: William Morrow & Co., 1976), 305.
33. Chervin, *Quotable Saints*, 102.
34. St. John of the Cross, 348-349.
35. *Marie of the Incarnation, Selected Writings*, 16.
36. *Marie of the Incarnation*, 17.
37. van Kaam, 53.
38. Goerres, *The Hidden Face*, 375.

SEVEN
Meeting Christ in the Suffering of Loneliness and Loss

1. *Marie of the Incarnation: Selected Writings*, Introduction by Irene Mahoney, O.S.U., 8.
2. *Marie of the Incarnation*, 9-10.
3. *Marie of the Incarnation*, 10-11.
4. *Marie of the Incarnation*, 14.
5. *Marie of the Incarnation*, 221ff.
6. *Marie of the Incarnation*, 17.
7. *Marie of the Incarnation*, 149.
8. *Marie of the Incarnation*, 153.
9. *Marie of the Incarnation*, 156.
10. St. Augustine, *Confessions*, translated with an introduction by R.S. Pine-Coffin (London: Penguin Books, 1961), 75-81.
11. Ratisbonne, 41ff.
12. Ratisbonne, 41ff.
13. Ratisbonne, 426.
14. Ratisbonne, 201.
15. Fr. Bruno, 230-232.
16. Fr. Bruno, 231.
17. Eddie Doherty, *Martin* (New York: Sheed and Ward, 1948), 8-9.
18. Beahn, *A Man Born Again*, 116.
19. Francis de Sales and Jane de Chantal, *Letters*, 74.
20. Francis de Sales and Jane de Chantal, *Letters*, 74.
21. Charmot, 57.
22. Francis de Sales and Jane de Chantal, *Letters*, 76.
23. Chervin, *Quotable Saints*, 150.
24. Juliana Wadham, *The Case of Cornelia Connelly* (New York: Pantheon, 1957), 37-38.
25. *Conchita: A Mother's Spiritual Diary*, edited by M.M. Philipon, O.P., translated by Aloysius J. Owens, S.J. (Staten Island: Alba House, 1978).
26. *Conchita*, 49-51.
27. Fr. Martin-Maria Olive, 103-105.

EIGHT
Meeting Christ in the Suffering of Marital Discord

1. Wadham.
2. Wadham, 39-41.
3. Wadham, 40.
4. Wadham, 41.
5. Wadham, 102.
6. Wadham, 114.
7. Wadham, 116.
8. Wadham, 119.

9. Wadham, 120.
10. Wadham, 143.
11. Wadham, 145.
12. Chervin, *A Treasury of Women Saints*, 325.
13. Chervin, *A Treasury of Women Saints*, 243-244.
14. Chervin, *A Treasury of Women Saints*, 6-7.
15. Chervin, *A Treasury of Women Saints*, 59-60.
16. Rev. M.J. Corcoran, O.S.A., *Our Own St. Rita* (New York: Benziger Brothers, 1919), 60.
17. Mother Mary G. Duffin, *A Heroine of Charity: Venerable Mother d'Youville* (New York: Benziger Brothers, 1938), 33-37.
18. Duffin, 36.

NINE
Meeting Christ in the Suffering of Persecution

1. Bruno, 133.
2. Bruno, 158ff.
3. Bruno, 171.
4. Bruno, 175.
5. Bruno, 179.
6. Bruno, 185.
7. Bruno, 305.
8. Bruno, 344.
9. Bruno, 78.
10. Chervin, *Treasury of Women Saints*, 156.
11. Chervin, *Prayers of the Women Mystics* (Ann Arbor, Mich.: Servant, 1992), 91-100.
12. Twain, Mark *Joan of Arc* (San Francisco: Ignatius, 1989), 341.
13. Twain, 343.
14. Beahn, 3.
15. Beahn, 5.
16. *Butler's Lives of the Saints*, Vol. III, 52-53.
17. Beahn, 208.
18. *Butler's Lives of the Saints*, Vol. IV, 282-283.
19. *Butler's Lives of the Saints*, 283.
20. James Anthony Walsh, *A Modern Martyr: Jean Theophane Venard* (New York: McMullen Books, Inc., 1952), 94-114.
21. Walsh, 100.
22. Walsh, 104.
23. Fanchon Royer, *Padre Pio* (New York: P.J. Kenedy and Sons, 1954).
24. Royer, 164.
25. Royer, 209.
26. Patricia Treece, *A Man for Others: Maximilian Kolbe, Saint of Auschwitz* (Huntington, Ind.: Our Sunday Visitor, 1982), 172-179.
27. Treece, 172.
28. von Matt and Hilpisch, 75.
29. Ratisbonne, 112.

30. Ratisbonne, 415.
31. Ratisbonne, 422.
32. See the quote from Joergensen's *Francis of Assisi* in Fr. Bruno's *Saint John of the Cross*, 79.
33. Joly, 80-81.
34. Joly, 173.
35. Joly, 251.
36. Bruno, 155.
37. For the life of Maria Goretti see Marie Cecilia Buehrle, *Saint Maria Goretti* (Milwaukee: The Bruce Publishing Company, 1950). For the life of Alessandro, see *The Penitent* by Pietro DiDonato (New York: Hawthorn Books, Inc., 1962).

TEN

Meeting Christ In the Suffering of Confrontation with Error

1. Beahn.
2. Beahn, 166.
3. *Butler's Lives of the Saints*, Vol. III, 52.
4. Beahn, 178.
5. *Butler*, Vol. III, 54.
6. Chervin, *Quotable Saints*, 86.
7. von Matt and Hilpisch.
8. von Matt and Hilpisch, 108.
9. von Matt and Hilpisch, 114.
10. von Matt and Hilpisch, 128.
11. Ratisbonne.
12. Ratisbonne, 331.
13. Ratisbonne, 250.
14. Ratisbonne, 262.
15. Ratisbonne, 272-273.
16. Pere Regamey, "The Five Beats of Every Apostolic Life," *Life of the Spirit*, March 1960, 406-409.
17. Joly, 201.
18. Chervin, *Quotable Saints*, 112.

ELEVEN

Meeting Christ in the Suffering of Physical Pain and Fatigue

1. J.K. Huysmans, *Saint Lydwine of Scheidam*, translated by Agnes Hastings (Rockford, Ill.: Tan, 1979).
2. Huysmans, iv.
3. Huysmans, 47.
4. Huysmans, 49-54.
5. Huysmans, 58.
6. Huysmans, 60ff.

7. Huysmans, 67.
8. Huysmans, 68.
9. Huysmans, 68.
10. Huysmans, 114ff.
11. Huysmans, 114.
12. Huysmans, 76.
13. Huysmans, 92-94.
14. Huysmans, 108-110.
15. Huysmans, 123.
16. Huysmans, 193.
17. Huysmans, 200.
18. Ratisbonne, 76.
19. Ratisbonne, 317.
20. Ratisbonne, 375.
21. St. Teresa, 281.
22. St. Teresa, 362.
23. Bruno, 316.
24. Treece, 25.
25. Treece, 46-47.
26. Treece, 47.
27. Treece, 128ff.
28. Treece, 141.

TWELVE
Meeting Christ in the Suffering of Temptation

1. Raymond of Capua, *Catherine of Siena*, translated by Conleth Kearns, O.P. (Wilmington, DE: Michael Glazier, 1980).
2. Raymond, 29-30.
3. Raymond, 52.
4. Raymond, 56-57.
5. Raymond, 96-109.
6. Catherine of Siena, *The Dialogue*, translated by Suzanne Noffke, O.P. (New York: Paulist Press, 1980).
7. Catherine, 132.
8. Catherine, 142.
9. Catherine, 168.
10. Catherine, 189.
11. Catherine, 87-88.
12. Brown, 58.
13. Brown, 100-102.
14. Chervin, *Quotable Saints*, 202-203.
15. Chervin, *Quotable Saints*, 204.
16. von Matt and Hilpisch, 70.
17. von Matt and Hilpisch, 183.
18. Chervin, *Quotable Saints*, 100.

19. Ratisbonne, 29.
20. Joly, 19.
21. St. Teresa, 297.
22. Bruno, 133.
23. Doherty, 183-185.
24. *Marie of the Incarnation: Selected Writings*, 103ff.
25. Doherty, *Matt Talbot* (Milwaukee: The Bruce Publishing Company, 1953), 43ff.
26. Concepcion Cabrera De Armida, *Before the Altar* (Mexico: Ediciones Cimien to, 1988), 115-116.

Bibliography

Beahn, John Edward. *A Man Born Again: Saint Thomas More.* Milwaukee: The Bruce Publishing Company, 1954.

Blessed Josemaria Escriva. Rome: Opus Dei, 1992.

Brown, Raphael. *The Life of Mary as Seen by the Mystics.* Milwaukee: The Bruce Publishing Company, 1951.

Bruno, O.D.C. *St. John of the Cross.* London: Sheed & Ward, 1936.

Buehrle, Marie Cecilia. *Saint Maria Goretti.* Milwaukee: The Bruce Publishing Company, 1950.

Catherine of Siena. *The Dialogue,* translated by Suzanne Noffke, O.P. Mahwah, N.J.: Paulist Press, 1980.

Cavnar, Cindy. *Prayers and Meditations of Therese of Lisieux.* Ann Arbor, Mich.: Servant, 1993.

Charmot, Francois, S.J. *Ignatius Loyola and Francis de Sales.* St. Louis: B. Herder, 1966.

Chervin, Ronda. *Prayers of the Women Mystics.* Ann Arbor, Mich.: Servant, 1992, *Quotable Saints.* Ann Arbor, Mich.: Servant, 1992, *Treasury of Women Saints.* Ann Arbor, Mich.: Servant, 1991, *Woman to Woman.* San Francisco: Ignatius Press, 1990.

Chesterton, G.K. *St. Francis of Assisi.* London: Hodder and Stoughton..

Corcoran, Rev. M.J., O.S.A. *Our Own St. Rita.* New York: Benziger Brothers, 1919.

De Armida, Concepcion Cabrera. *Before the Altar.* Mexico: Ediciones Cimiento, 1988.

De La Gorce, Agnes. *Saint Benedict Joseph Labre* translated by Rosemary Sheed. New York: Sheed and Ward, 1952.

DiDonato, Pietro. *The Penitent.* New York: Hawthorn Books, Inc., 1962.

Doherty, Eddie. *Martin.* New York: Sheed and Ward, 1948.

Doherty, Eddie. *Matt Talbot.* Milwaukee: The Bruce Publishing Company, 1953.

Duffin, Mother Mary G. *A Heroine of Charity: Venerable Mother d'Youville.* New York: Benziger Brothers, 1938.

Francis de Sales and Jane de Chantal. *Letters of Spiritual Direction,* translated by Peronne Marie Thibert, V.H.M. New York: Paulist Press, 1988.

Garvin, Paul, translator and editor,.*The Life and Sayings of Saint Catherine of Genoa,* Staten Island: Alba House, 1964.

Goerres, Ida. *The Hidden Face: A Study of St. Therese of Lisieux,* translated by Richard and Clara Winston. New York: Pantheon, 1959.

Przywara, Erich, S.J., editor. *The Heart of Newman,* Springfield, Ill.: Templegate, 1963.

Huysmans, J.K. *Saint Lydwine of Schiedam* translated by Agnes Hastings. Rockford, Ill.: Tan, 1979.

Joly, Henri, S.J. *Saint Ignatius of Loyola,* translated by Mildred Patridge. London: Duckworth and Co., 1899.

Magaret, Helene. *A Kingdom and a Cross: St. Alphonsus Liguori.* Milwaukee: The Bruce Publishing Co., 1958.

Mahoney, Irene, editor, *Marie of the Incarnation: Selected Writings,* O.S.U. New York: Paulist Press, 1989.

Martindale, C.C., S.J. *Life of Saint Camillus.* New York: Sheed and Ward, 1946.

Matt, Leon von and Hilpisch, Dom Stephan, O.S.B. *Saint Benedict* translated by Dom Ernest Graf, O.S.B. Chicago: Henry Regnery, 1961.

Neill, Mary, O.P. and Chervin, Ronda. *Great Saints, Great Friends.* Staten Island: Alba House, 1990, 136.

Newman, John Henry Cardinal. *Apologia Pro Vita Sua.* New York: Modern Library, 1950.

Olive, Father Martin-Maria O.P. *Praxedes: Wife, Mother, Widow and Lay Dominican* translated by Sister Maria Maez, O.P. Rockford, Ill.: Tan, 1980.

Philipon, M.M., O.P., editor. *Conchita, A Mother's Spiritual Diary,* translated by Aloysius J. Owens, S.J. Staten Island: Alba House, 1978.

Ratisbonne, Theodore. *St. Bernard of Clairvaux.* Rockford, Ill.: Tan, 1991.

Raymond of Capua. *The Life of Catherine of Siena* translated by Conleth Kearns, O.P. Wilmington, DE: Michael Glazier, 1980.

Royer, Fanchon. *Padre Pio.* New York: P.J. Kenedy and Sons, 1954.

Ruiz, Federico, O.C.D. *God Speaks in the Night: The Life, Times and*

Teaching of St. John of the Cross, translated by Kieran Kavanaugh, O.C.D. Washington, D.C.: I.C.S., 1991).

St. Alphonsus de Liguori. *The Sermons of St. Alphonsus Liguori.* Rockford, Ill.: Tan, 1982.

Saint Augustine. *Confessions* translated with an introduction by R.S. Pine-Coffin. London: Penguin Books, 1961.

St. John of the Cross. *Collected Works*, translated by Kieran Kavanaugh, O.C.D. and Otilio Rodriguez, O.C.D. Washington, D.C.: ICS Publications, 1979.

St. Teresa of Avila. *Collected Works*, translated by Otilio Rodriguez, O.C.D. and Kieran Kavanaugh, O.C.D. Washington, D.C.: ICS Publications, Vol. 1, 1976, Vol. II, 1980.

Scott, Paul. *The Raj Quartet.* New York: William Morrow & Co., 1976.

Spink, Kathryn. *I Need Souls Like You.* San Francisco: Harper and Row, 1984.

Thurston, Herbert J., S.J. and Donald Attwater, editors. *Butler's Lives of the Saints*, in 4 Volumes: Westminster, Md.: Christian Classics, 1981.

Treece, Patricia. *A Man for Others: Maximilian Kolbe, Saint of Auschwitz.* Huntington, Ind.: Our Sunday Visitor, Inc., 1982.

van Kaam, Adrian L., C.S.Sp. *A Light to the Gentiles: The Life-Story of the Venerable Francis Libermann.* Pittsburgh: Duquesne University, 1959.

Wadham, Juliana. *The Case of Cornelia Connelly.* New York: Pantheon, 1957.

Walsh, James Anthony. *A Modern Martyr: Jean Theophane Venard.* New York: McMullen Books, Inc., 1952.

Woodgate, Mildred Violet. *St. Louise de Marillac.* St. Louis: B. Herder, 1942.

Another Book of Interest to Servant Readers

Prayers of the Women Mystics

Ronda De Sola Chervin

"Praise to you, Spirit of Fire! to you who send the timbrel and lyre. Your music sets our mind ablaze. The strength of our souls awaits your coming in the tent of meeting."

—Hildegard of Bingen

This lyrical and imaginative prayer invoking the Holy Spirit was penned by a famous medieval mystic and is but a sample of the many stirring prayers in this collection. Journey in prayer with great women mystics and through the prism of mystical prayer, glimpse their profound intimacy with God. Gertrude the Great, Birgitta of Sweden, Julian of Norwich, Catherine of Siena, Teresa of Avila, and fourteen mystics are included.

Each chapter on a particular mystic includes commentary on her life and spirituality and a selection of prayers organized by key themes. *Prayers of the Women Mystics* will appeal to all Christians who desire deeper intimacy with God, especially those attracted to mystical experience and prayer. *$7.99*

Available at your Christian bookstore or from:
Servant Publications • Dept. 209 • P.O. Box 7455
Ann Arbor, Michigan 48107
Please include payment plus $2.75 per book
for postage and handling.
*Send for our FREE catalog of Christian
books, music, and cassettes.*